fusion

3

Sam Holyman
Phil Routledge
David Sang

Series Editor: Lawrie Ryan

Nelson Thornes

Acknowledgements

The Pupil Book authors wish to express their special thanks to the following people

Neil Roscoe	James Routledge
John Payne	Joel Routledge
Ruth Miller	Jack Routledge
Jane Taylor	Sarah Ryan
Judy Ryan	Amanda Wilson
Paul Lister	Annie Hamblin
Nick Pollock	Doug Thompson
Darren Forbes	Geoff Covey
Geoff Carr	Claire Gordon
Bev Routledge	

Published in 2009 by:
Nelson Thornes Ltd
Delta Place
27 Bath Road
CHELTENHAM
GL53 7TH
United Kingdom

09 10 11 12 / 10 9 8 7 6 5 4 3 2 1

A catalogue record for this book is available from the British Library

ISBN 978 0 7487 9839 1

Illustrations by GreenGate Publishing, Barking Dog Art, Harry Venning and Roger Penwill

Cover photograph: Photolibrary

Page make-up by GreenGate Publishing Services, Tonbridge, Kent

Printed and bound in Croatia by Zrinski

Contents

Introduction

What is this book about?

By the time you read this you will have found out lots of exciting things from Fusion 1 and 2. Just like the first two Fusion books, this book aims to give **you** the ideas and knowledge to challenge the world around you. There are lots of fun and interesting practical ideas included here to keep you switched on to science.

Building on the skills and knowledge you learned in Fusion 2, this book will help you to see the connections between the different areas of science. It will also help you to apply the skills you have practised to new situations.

Fusion 3 will take you through lots of everyday applications of science. You've probably heard about global warming, cloning and the destruction of rainforests. Well now you will learn the science behind these topics, and discuss answers to lots of other burning questions! Are GM crops a good thing? How do you stop a bee sting hurting? What does smoking do to you? Should we have nuclear energy? How do speed cameras work? Science will take you beyond the classroom, and you will learn why science is important for your own life as well as how scientists and science have an impact on the whole planet.

Next time you...

... run to catch the bus, make toast, eat sherbet, see lightning, you can link your science knowledge to what you are seeing or doing. It's a great way to remind yourself of what you know.

Link up to...

Another subject. It could be History, Geography, Design and Technology or any others that you study. Lots of subjects have ideas and skills that overlap.

Stretch Yourself

Some bits of science are easier to understand than others. If you find an area of science easy you might want to stretch yourself by trying some harder tasks.

The Fusion team are passionate about science, and not just because we think it's fun, exciting and hands on! Learning science gives you life skills too, such as investigating problems or issues, making your own conclusions based on evidence, working as part of a team, and communicating your ideas to other people. These are useful skills for studying any subject, but they are also really valuable in your personal life and eventually your working life too.

Just like the other two Fusion books, there are lots of features in this book to help you. Examples of these are shown on the left and overleaf. You are on the final part of your Fusion journey, so strap yourself in and get ready for a fantastic fusion of all the best bits of science…enjoy the ride!

Help Yourself

Some bits of science are difficult to understand and you may need a bit of help. This feature gives you tips and shows you connections that may make it all easier to understand.

activity

Activity

Science is a very practical subject and we have tried to make this book as active as possible. The activities in this book vary from full practical investigations to much smaller activities. They help to develop your knowledge and skills in as fun and active a way as possible.

Questions in the yellow boxes. These are quick questions to check that you understand the science you are learning.

Summary Questions

These check that you understand everything. Some questions are easy to answer. Others are more challenging and you may need to ask for help. You can use questions to help see what you understand well and to see where you can improve.

KEY WORDS

Important scientific words are shown in bold and appear in a list on the page and in the glossary at the back of the book.

Health

NEW

Nutty Cornflakes

NUTRITION INFORMATION PER 100 g

ENERGY	1700 kJ 400 kcal
PROTEIN	7.0 g
CARBOHYDRATE	83 g
of which sugars	35 g
starch	48 g
FAT	4.0 g
of which saturates	0.8 g
SODIUM	0.8 g
FIBRE	1.0 g
VITAMINS:	
NIACIN	15 mg
VITAMIN B$_6$	1.8 mg
RIBOFLAVIN(B$_2$)	1.5 mg
THIAMIN(B$_1$)	1.0 mg
FOLIC ACID	250 µg
VITAMIN D	2.8 µg
VITAMIN B$_{12}$	1.7 µg
IRON	6.7 mg

Baked Beans are rich in fibre and protein and form a valuable part of a nutritious and well balanced diet.

Baked Beans in a rich tomato sauce. Delicious hot or cold, at breakfast, lunch and dinner.

NUTRITION INFORMATION
100 g provides

ENERGY	280 kJ/66 kcal
PROTEIN	5.0 g
CARBOHYDRATE	11.0 g
(of which sugars	5.0 g)
FAT	0.5 g
(of which saturates	0.1 g)
SODIUM	0.5 g
FIBRE	7.3 g

Health

There are many factors that can affect our health:

- the amount and types of foods we eat
- the amount of exercise we take
- drugs, including drinking alcohol and smoking tobacco
- microbes.

What we eat

Foods contain carbohydrates, protein, fats, vitamins, minerals, fibre and water. We need all of these in a balanced diet. Can you remember how to test foods to identify some of them?

Luckily we do not need to test our food to find out what it contains! Most foods have labels that list the amount of different nutrients.

NUTRITION: **Sardines** in brine are a source of Calcium and Vitamin D, both needed for strong bones and teeth; Vitamin B$_{12}$ required for healthy blood and nervous system, Niacin which helps food to give us energy.	TYPICAL VALUES PER 100 g (3 1/2 oz) OF DRAINED PRODUCT
ENERGY	170 kCALORIES 705 kJOULES
PROTEIN	23.4 g
CARBOHYDRATE	less than 0.1 g
TOTAL FAT	8.3 g
ADDED SALT	0.5 g
VITAMINS/ MINERALS	% OF RECOMMENDED DAILY AMOUNT
NIACIN	45%
VITAMIN B$_{12}$	1400%
VITAMIN D	300%
CALCIUM	110%
IRON	25%

a Which food, from the labels shown, gives you the most energy per 100 g?

b Which food contains the most protein?

c Which food contains the least fat?

(d) Why is the information given per 100 g of food? Is this always helpful?

(e) The sardines and the cornflakes use different methods of showing the amount of vitamins. Explain what each method means. Which do you think is most helpful? Explain your answer.

Testing foods

If we are going to have a balanced diet we need to know what different foods contain. A balanced diet should contain carbohydrate (starch and sugar), protein and fat. You should already know how to carry out tests for these different nutrients.

Write a short paragraph to explain how to carry out each of these tests. Explain what result would show that the nutrient was present in the food.

Now test the foods that your teacher gives you.

Draw a table to display your results.

▷ **Safety:** Wear eye protection if doing the practical.

Exercise

Lots of people join gyms in an attempt to take exercise, but stop going after a few weeks. One reason they give is that they cannot find the time.

Exercise is important but it doesn't need to be like this

(f) Suggest some ways that people can fit exercise into their everyday routines.

Cycling to work or school is a good way of getting exercise

Genes

The genes you inherited from your parents have the biggest effect on your health. Unfortunately you cannot change your genes but you can make sure that you take any family history into account. For example, if a number of people in your family have suffered from heart disease you can have your cholesterol level checked by your doctor. If you know you have a high cholesterol level then you can modify your lifestyle or get drugs to reduce the level.

Balanced Diet

- Which foods are used as a source of energy?
- Why does our body need protein?
- What nutrients do we need in a healthy diet?
- How can I evaluate my investigation into the energy in food?

Energy and food

Food gives you the energy you need to keep your body going. Most of your energy comes from carbohydrates, which contain about 17 kJ/g. If your diet contains more energy than you use your body will store it as fat. This means you gain weight. Fats contain about 37 kJ/g, so if your diet is high in fat you are more likely to put on weight.

Your body needs energy for:

- keeping warm
- moving about
- growing
- repairing damaged tissues
- keeping your body processes going, such as breathing, digesting food, etc.
- growing a new baby.

Different people need different amounts of energy.

Person	Daily energy needed (kJ)
15 year-old girl	8900
15 year-old boy	9500
Female office worker	9500
Male office worker	11 500
Male bricklayer	15 000
Pregnant office worker	10 000

a Draw a bar chart of the information in the table.

b Why do you think males usually need more energy than females?

c Why does the bricklayer need more energy than the office worker?

d Why does a pregnant woman need more energy than a woman who is not pregnant?

Protein

Young people need protein in their diet as it is used for growth. It is also used for:

- making things like hair and fingernails
- repairing damaged and injured parts of the body
- replacing parts that are lost, such as skin cells and the cells lining the intestine
- making **antibodies** that help us to fight diseases
- making **hormones**
- making **enzymes** that control chemical reactions in the body.

Did You Know?

70–80% of household dust is actually made of skin cells! The average person loses about 300 g of skin cells per year.

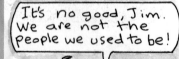

It's no good, Jim. We are not the people we used to be!

activity

Comparing the energy in food

We can find out how much energy is in food by burning it and measuring the amount of heat given off. As the food burns the energy is used to heat water. The more energy, the hotter the water gets.

- Measure out 20 cm³ of water into the boiling tube.
- Measure the temperature of the water.
- Use a Bunsen burner to light the food sample. Use the burning food to heat the water.
- When the food stops burning, stir the water and measure the temperature again.
- Calculate the rise in temperature.
- Repeat the experiment with other food samples. Use a table like this one to record your results.

Food	Temperature of the water at the start (°C)	Temperature of the water at the finish (°C)	Increase in temperature (°C)

- How did you make sure you carried out a fair test?
- How can you make your results more reliable?
- Did all of the energy go into the water? How could you improve the investigation?
- Which food contained the most energy?

⚠ **Safety:** Wear eye protection.

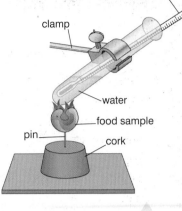

Measuring the energy in food

Fats

We often think that fats are unhealthy, but this is not true. Fats are needed to make all cell membranes. They are also essential for making brain and nerve cells. Some vitamins are mainly found in foods containing fats. **Too much fat** is unhealthy. A high fat diet contains a lot of energy so it increases the chances of gaining weight. It is also true that plant oils are usually better than fats from animals.

Great Debates

Many scientists believe that oils containing omega-3 fatty acids are very beneficial in improving our health. Some people think they help improve learning and behaviour in young people. Many scientists are concerned, however, that the benefits have not been tested in proper 'trials'.

Summary Questions

1. Make a poster to show which foods are the best sources of the main nutrients and how we use them in our body.

2. Find out about the benefits of eating foods containing omega-3 oils. Find out about how 'double blind' trials are used to test the benefits of new products.

KEY WORDS

antibody
hormone
enzyme

Malnutrition

> ▸▸ What are the causes of malnutrition?
>
> ▸▸ How can poor diet cause problems such as obesity and heart disease?

Malnutrition means 'bad nutrition'. Some people do not get enough food. This is one kind of malnutrition. The boy in the photograph is suffering from starvation due to famine.

Malnutrition due to famine

The boy in the photograph opposite is suffering from **kwashiorkor** caused by a lack of protein in the diet. A swollen belly is one of the symptoms of kwashiorkor.

> **ⓐ** What is the cause of kwashiorkor?

We often think that malnutrition is something that only occurs in poor countries during drought and famine. However it also happens in wealthy countries where there is plenty of food.

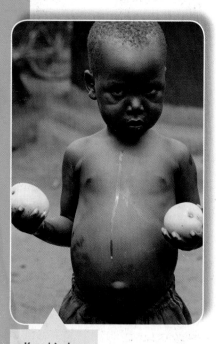
Kwashiorkor

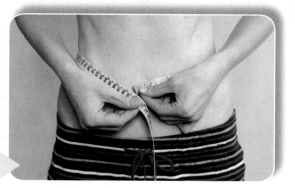
Anorexia

People like the young person in the photograph can end up in hospital because they are suffering from an eating disorder called **anorexia nervosa**. They are convinced that they are overweight and must lose more weight.

People who are anorexic do not eat enough food to keep them going. As well as becoming very thin, anorexics suffer many other serious health problems. About one anorexic in ten will die as a result of the condition.

> **ⓑ** What is anorexia nervosa?

If we take in more energy than we use then the excess is stored as body fat. We all need some body fat but if we have too much we become **obese**. This can cause many health problems:

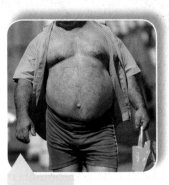

Obesity

Help Yourself

Smoking cigarettes and eating too much salt increase blood pressure. Taking regular exercise helps you to keep to a healthy weight and reduces your chances of having a heart attack.

- Fats are deposited in arteries, forming an **atheroma**. This makes the artery wall rough so blood does not flow smoothly. It also makes the artery narrower. Blood cells stick to the atheroma and form clots. These clots can reduce the flow of blood to the heart muscles causing a **coronary thrombosis** or heart attack. Clots in the brain can cause a **stroke**, where blood cannot reach parts of the brain.
- Extra body mass puts a strain on the joints, which can cause **arthritis**.
- Obesity is often linked to people developing diabetes in middle age.

Cholesterol is essential for making cell membranes, but too much 'bad' cholesterol increases the risk of narrowing of the arteries. Animal fats tend to produce 'bad' cholesterol, while plant oils produce 'good' cholesterol.

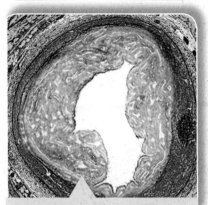

The yellow layer is an atheroma

Balancing diets

- Keep a record of everything you eat and drink for a day. Try to estimate the size of the portions you eat. Don't forget any snacks or sweets you eat between meals!
- Make a record of all of the activities you do during the day. Include any time when you are walking, running, doing PE, or just sitting relaxing.
- Use food labels, books of 'food tables' and the internet to help you to work out your energy intake for the day. Make a table to show what you ate and how much energy it contained.
- Use information about the energy used in different activities to work out how much energy you used in the day.
- Make a table or chart to compare your energy intake and energy output.

Fibre

Fibre is mainly made of plant cell walls. We cannot digest fibre but it is an important part of our diet. It absorbs water which makes faeces softer and easier to move along the intestines. Without fibre we become constipated. It is thought that fibre has other benefits including reducing cholesterol levels, preventing bowel cancer and improving the immune system.

Summary Questions

1. Phil is overweight, he has high blood pressure and his cholesterol level is too high. His doctor has told him he is at risk of having a heart attack. Draw up a diet plan for Phil.

KEY WORDS

malnutrition
kwashiorkor
anorexia nervosa
obese
atheroma
coronary thrombosis
stroke
arthritis

Vitamins and Minerals

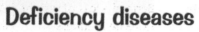

- ▶▶ Why do we need vitamins and minerals?
- ▶▶ Which foods are good sources of vitamins and minerals?
- ▶▶ How did scientists discover the importance of vitamins in our diet?

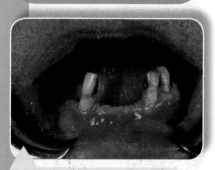

Scurvy causes bleeding gums and loss of teeth

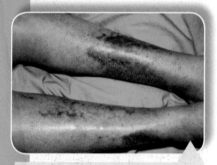

Scurvy causes bleeding leg ulcers

Did You Know?

In 1740 a British expedition set off to sail around the world. Of 1900 men who started the voyage, 1400 died, mostly from scurvy.

Deficiency diseases

Before 1800, sailors often suffered from a disease called 'scurvy'. It caused bleeding, loss of teeth and hair, depression, blindness and death. Sailors often spent weeks away from land and rarely got fresh fruit or vegetables. Their diet mainly consisted of salted meat and ship's biscuits, often containing maggots and insects!

Some people believed that scurvy was prevented by eating citrus fruits, such as lemons and oranges. A naval surgeon called James Lind thought that it was the acid in citrus fruit that actually prevented scurvy. In 1747 he carried out an investigation to test his idea. This was an early example of a **clinical trial**.

He took 12 sailors who were suffering from scurvy. He divided them into pairs. They were all given the same diet but each pair was given an extra supplement every day. After a week the sailors were examined. Here are the results of his investigation:

Pair	Daily dietary supplement	Effect noticed after one week
A	Two pints of cider	Slight recovery
B	25 drops of sulfuric acid	No effect
C	6 spoons of vinegar	No effect
D	Half a pint of seawater	No effect
E	Two oranges and one lemon	One sailor fully recovered and one almost recovered
F	Spicy paste and barley water	No effect

In the years that followed, lemon or lime juice was added to sailors' diets and they did not suffer from scurvy.

> **ⓐ** Why did sailors suffer from scurvy more than other groups of people?

> **ⓑ** Why did James Lind give some of the sailors vinegar or sulfuric acid?

> **ⓒ** Why did group E recover from scurvy?

> **ⓓ** Why did group A show slight recovery?

Vitamins and minerals

James Lind did not know about vitamins, but we now know that citrus fruits contain **vitamin** C. Vitamins are chemical compounds. Our body needs small amounts of vitamins to function properly. Without vitamins we will suffer from a **deficiency disease**. Our body also needs small amounts of **minerals** to work properly. See the following table.

Nutrient	How it is used by our body	Deficiency disease	Good sources
Vitamin A	For healthy skin and good night vision	Night blindness	Dairy products, oily fish, carrots, green vegetables
Vitamin B1	Healthy nerves and for the release of energy from foods	Beriberi – loss of weight, extreme tiredness	Wholegrain cereal, yeast, eggs, nuts, liver, peas and beans
Vitamin C	Protection of cells, absorption of iron	Scurvy	Citrus fruits, blackcurrants, salad, tomatoes, kiwi fruit
Vitamin D	Absorption of calcium	Rickets	Oily fish, milk, cheese, butter, margarine, eggs. It is also made in the skin when it is sunny
Calcium	Making bones and teeth, needed for nerves to function	Rickets	Cheese, milk, butter, sardines, bread, spinach, chocolate
Iron	Carrying oxygen in the red blood cells	Anaemia	Liver, red meat, eggs, cereals, apricots, spinach, cocoa

activity

Testing foods for vitamin C

We can use a chemical called DCPIP to measure the vitamin C content of food. DCPIP is blue but it is decolourised by vitamin C.

- Put 1 cm^3 of DCPIP in a test tube.
- Measure 2 cm^3 of freshly squeezed orange juice into a syringe.
- Add drops of orange juice to the DCPIP until the blue colour has disappeared.
- Record the number of drops of orange juice needed to decolourise the DCPIP.
- Compare the amount of vitamin C in freshly squeezed orange juice with different brands of orange juice in cartons, or with different citrus fruits such as lemon, lime and grapefruit.

Beriberi

Rickets

Great Debates

Sir Frederick Gowland Hopkins used rats in experiments that made significant discoveries about the importance of vitamins. Many rats died in his experiments. Should scientists be allowed to use animals in experiments?

Summary Questions

1. Why do we need iron in our diet?

2. Why does a seven-year old need more calcium than his dad?

3. Why do teenage girls need more iron than teenage boys?

4. Use pictures from magazines and the internet to make a poster about the importance of vitamins and minerals.

KEY WORDS

clinical trial
vitamin
deficiency disease
mineral

Smoking

- ▸▸ What is tobacco smoke made of?
- ▸▸ How do the substances in cigarette smoke affect us?
- ▸▸ How did scientists find out about the harm caused by cigarette smoke?

Our lungs and airways are lined with special epithelial cells. Dirt and microbes stick to the **mucus** produced by **goblet cells**. **Cilia** brush the mucus with its trapped dirt and microbes to the back of the throat where it is swallowed. Acid in the stomach kills the microbes.

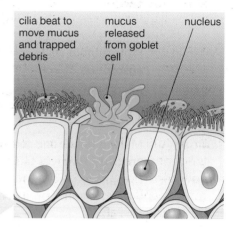

cilia beat to move mucus and trapped debris

mucus released from goblet cell

nucleus

Cells lining the airways

Healthy people have millions of tiny air sacs called alveoli. These give the lungs a large surface area so that we can absorb plenty of oxygen and remove the carbon dioxide produced in respiration.

ⓐ What is the job of the cilia?

ⓑ Why is it important that alveoli give the lungs a large surface area?

What's in tobacco smoke?

activity

Investigating cigarette smoke

- Turn on the pump for five minutes without a cigarette in the machine.
- Observe the temperature, the colour of the limewater and the appearance of the glass wool.
- Repeat the experiment, this time with a lit cigarette in the machine.
- Record your observations.

⚠ **Safety:** This 'machine' must only be used in a fume cupboard.

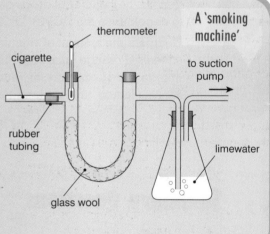

A 'smoking machine'

thermometer

cigarette

to suction pump

rubber tubing

glass wool

limewater

Cigarette smoke contains hundreds of different chemicals but the main ones are:

- **Nicotine** – an **addictive** substance. Once you start smoking it is very difficult to stop. Nicotine causes high blood pressure.
- **Carbon monoxide** – combines with haemoglobin in your red blood cells, reducing the amount of oxygen your blood can carry. It also damages the cilia.

- **Tars** – a number of different chemicals, including some which cause cancer.
- **Carbon** – small particles in smoke which make you cough and also cause cancer.
- **Hot gases** – high temperatures damage cilia.

What does smoking do to you?

Smoking causes a number of diseases and health problems:

- **Lung cancer** – caused by many of the chemicals in smoke.
- **Emphysema** – damage to the alveoli reduces the surface area of the alveoli.
- **Bronchitis** – damage to the cilia means that microbes stay in the lungs and are more likely to start an infection.
- **Low birth weight** – if a pregnant woman smokes the fetus does not get enough oxygen. This increases the chances of having an underweight baby.
- **Smoker's cough** – to remove mucus from the lungs as the cilia are damaged.

> **c** Make a table summarising the health problems caused by smoking.

Healthy lung (left) and smoker's lung (right)

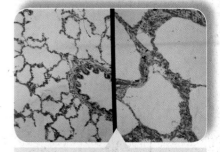

Normal lung (left) and lung with emphysema (right) seen through a microscope

How did we find out that smoking was bad for us?

Fifty years ago smoking was very common. It wasn't unusual to see sportsmen smoking or even advertising cigarettes. In the 1950s people started to see links between smoking and diseases, especially lung cancer. It was difficult to prove the

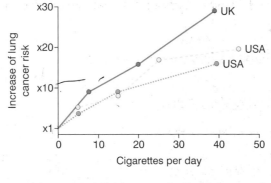

A graph showing statistics linking smoking and disease

link, however, as scientists could not experiment on people. Some experiments were carried out on animals but the main evidence about the dangers of smoking came from careful study of statistics.

Did You Know?

Smoking causes about 120 000 deaths per year in the UK, about 20% of the total.

Summary Questions

1. Produce a poster or leaflet, aimed at young people, explaining about the dangers of smoking.

2. Cigarettes cost about £5.50 for 20. Calculate the annual cost of smoking 10 cigarettes per day.

3. People's attitudes to smoking have changed over the years. Carry out a survey to find out why people start smoking, whether they support the ban on smoking in public places, why people find it hard to give up smoking, etc.

KEY WORDS

mucus
goblet cell
cilia
nicotine
addictive
carbon monoxide
tar
carbon
lung cancer
emphysema
bronchitis

Alcohol

- ▸ How does alcohol affect your body?
- ▸ How does alcohol affect your behaviour?
- ▸ What is a 'unit' of alcohol?
- ▸ How does alcohol affect an unborn baby?

A good night out?

How does alcohol affect your behaviour?

Alcohol affects your nervous system. When you drink alcohol it is absorbed from your stomach into your bloodstream. It is quickly carried to your brain. At first you feel cheerful, but alcohol is a depressant. You might start to feel more emotional, your speech starts to become slurred and your vision is affected.

Soon you lose coordination – you can't walk without stumbling but you still feel great! Your judgement is not so good and you might do things you regret. You might be sick and could choke. A few drinks more and you are in a state of **stupor**. You do not know where you are or what you are doing. This can be followed by coma.

Reaction time

Alcohol is a **depressant,** which means it slows down your reaction times. It takes an average driver about 0.75 seconds from seeing danger to putting their foot on the brake pedal. Four units of alcohol will increase this time by about 0.25 seconds.

a A car is moving at 20 m/s. A pedestrian steps into the road. How far will the car travel in the 0.75 seconds it takes the driver to react?

b How much further will the car travel if the driver has had two pints of beer?

c What is meant by being 'over the limit'?

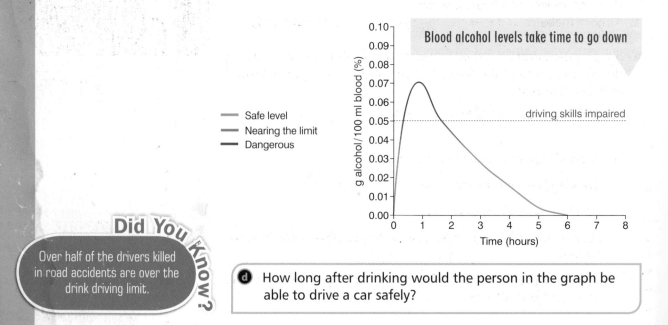

d How long after drinking would the person in the graph be able to drive a car safely?

Units of alcohol

The more alcohol a person drinks, the more and the quicker it affects them. Different alcoholic drinks contain different amounts of alcohol. One way to compare the strength of different drinks is to compare how many **units of alcohol** they contain.

The recommended maximum is:

- Men: 21 units per week and no more than 4 units per day.
- Women: 14 units per week and no more than 4 units per day.

| small bottle of beer | 1 small glass of vodka | 1 bottle of 'alcopop' | 1 small glass of wine | ¹/₂ pint of cider |

Each of these drinks contains one unit of alcohol

It takes about one hour to remove one unit of alcohol from the body.

How does alcohol affect your body?

- Alcohol is a drug. People can become addicted to alcohol. They are called **alcoholics**.
- Alcohol is a poison. Your liver breaks down poisons in your body. Drinking too much alcohol over a number of years causes **cirrhosis** of the liver. The liver is damaged and cannot do its job properly.
- Alcohol can cause stomach ulcers, brain damage, mouth and stomach cancer and heart disease.
- Alcohol makes blood vessels in the skin open up so your body cools down.
- If a pregnant woman drinks, some of the alcohol will pass into the blood stream of the fetus. This can interfere with its growth and development.

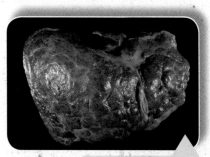

Liver with cirrhosis

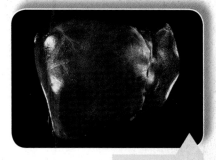

Healthy liver

Summary Questions

1. Answer true or false to these statements:

   Drinking black coffee sobers you up.

   Drinking whisky warms you up.

   People will find you more likeable when you have been drinking alcohol.

2. Make a leaflet aimed at people your age, giving them information about drinking alcohol.

KEY WORDS

depressant
unit of alcohol
alcoholic
cirrhosis

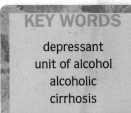

Drugs

- ▶▶ What is meant by a drug?
- ▶▶ What are the ways in which drugs are used?
- ▶▶ How do drugs affect your body?
- ▶▶ How can I plan an investigation into caffeine and reaction time?

Drugs ▶

Are drugs harmful?

Alcohol is a drug. So is caffeine, found in cola drinks, tea and coffee. We take painkillers containing paracetemol, another drug. So what do we mean when we talk about drugs?

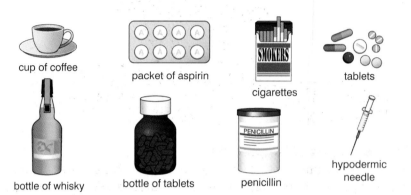

cup of coffee

packet of aspirin

cigarettes

tablets

bottle of whisky

bottle of tablets

penicillin

hypodermic needle

A **drug** is a substance that changes the way your body works. If you are ill your doctor might prescribe drugs or you might buy them at the chemist or supermarket. Drugs that help you get better are called **therapeutic drugs**. It is important that therapeutic drugs are taken in carefully controlled amounts. They can cause harm if too big a dose is taken.

activity

Caffeine and reaction time

Investigate the effect of caffeine on reaction times. There are various ways of measuring reaction times. Try to measure a person's reaction times before and after drinking a cola drink containing caffeine.

- How will you make sure your investigation is reliable?
- How will you make sure your investigation is a fair test?

a Painkillers are therapeutic drugs. Name some other types of therapeutic drug.

Recreational drugs

People take **recreational drugs** because they enjoy the effect they have on their bodies. Tobacco and alcohol are recreational drugs. Many people enjoy using them but, as we have already seen, they cause serious health problems. You can only buy them when you are over a certain age.

b What age do you have to be to buy alcohol and tobacco?

c What other laws control the use of alcohol and tobacco?

Other recreational drugs are illegal. These include cannabis, ecstasy, LSD, heroin, cocaine and amphetamines. People also sniff things like the **solvents** in some types of glue and lighter fuel.

How do drugs affect people?

Some drugs are **addictive**. Your body develops a physical need for the drug and you feel ill without it. Without the drug, addicts get cravings. They need to take more of the drug just to get rid of the craving.

Recreational drugs affect the body in different ways:

- **Depressants** slow down the nervous system – alcohol, lighter fuel, solvents (including glue) and tranquillisers.
- **Stimulants** speed up the nervous system – amphetamines, cocaine and ecstasy.
- **Hallucinogens** change the way you see and hear things – cannabis, 'magic' mushrooms and LSD.
- **Analgesics** are painkillers – heroin.

Taking too much of a drug can cause an **overdose**. This can cause permanent harm to the body, or even death. It is impossible to know how strong illegal drugs are so it is easy to take an overdose.

Drugs are usually expensive. People often turn to crime to get the money to buy drugs.

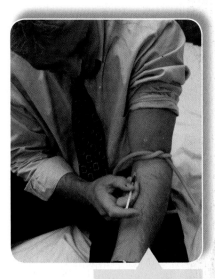

Injecting drugs

How do people take drugs?

There are several different ways of taking drugs. Some, such as ecstasy and amphetamines, are swallowed as tablets. Some, such as cannabis, are smoked. Some drugs, like heroin, are injected. If users share needles they risk passing on infections such as hepatitis and HIV.

Summary Questions

1 Make a display about different kinds of drug. Sort them into those that are legal, illegal, legal with age limits and legal with a prescription. Describe how the drug is taken. What type of drug is it and what are its effects on the body? Find out about the penalties for possessing and using each drug.

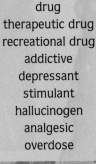

KEY WORDS

drug
therapeutic drug
recreational drug
addictive
depressant
stimulant
hallucinogen
analgesic
overdose

Healthy Living

- ▶▶ How can exercise improve your health?
- ▶▶ How can exercise help develop muscles?
- ▶▶ How can inappropriate exercise cause damage?

How much exercise do you do? You should be aiming to do at least 60 minutes of moderate physical activity every day. That might sound a lot, but it doesn't mean you need to spend an hour a day working out in the gym or jogging.

Moderate physical activity includes any exercise that makes you feel warmer than normal and increases your pulse and breathing rate. You could probably fit a lot of activity into your normal routine. You could try walking or biking to school instead of taking the bus or getting a lift. You could play games at break time instead of just sitting around.

Physical activity does not just mean sport. Dancing is just as good an exercise as jogging (and many people think it is more fun!). This type of exercise is called 'aerobic' exercise. This means that your muscles are getting plenty of oxygen while you exercise.

ⓐ Draw up a 60 minute daily exercise programme for yourself. Include activities which can easily form part of your daily routine.

Dancing

Rollerskating

Jogging

Football

Cycling

What are the benefits of aerobic exercise?

- Aerobic exercise requires energy. This means it helps keep your weight balanced.
- It is very good for your **cardiovascular system** – that's your heart and blood vessels. It helps prevent the build up of fat deposits in the arteries and reduces the risk of heart disease.
- It helps to maintain healthy lungs and reduces the risk of asthma.
- Exercise helps to build strong bones.
- Exercising is a good way of overcoming boredom, can help you make new friends and is good for your mental health.

b Give some examples of aerobic exercise.

Link up to....

PE

It is important that you get some help from a PE teacher or sports coach before starting an aerobic exercise. You should also build up gradually as you develop your muscles.

activity

Exercise for health

Imagine you are setting up a fitness club. Work out an exercise programme for one of the following people:

- A 14 year-old girl who hates PE.
- A busy mum with two children aged 3 and 6.
- An office worker who works 2 miles from home.

Stretching, strength and suppleness

Different types of exercise help to build strong muscles, increase your strength and make your body more supple. This improves your posture, improves the shape of your body, helps you to do everyday activities without aches and pain and helps develop strong bones and joints.

Inappropriate exercise can damage joints and muscles. You just need to visit a hospital casualty department on a Saturday to see that!

c Give some examples of activities that:

(i) help develop muscles   (ii) increase suppleness.

Summary Questions

1 Make a leaflet explaining to people of your age why it is important to do moderate physical exercise every day.

2 Draw a flow chart to explain why your pulse rate and breathing rate increase when you exercise.

KEY WORDS

cardiovascular system

Too Small to See

My new boyfriend is a mushroom.

That seems a bit odd.

Yes, but he's a fun guy.

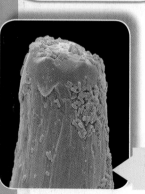

Bacteria on the point of a pin

Microbes are the smallest living things. They can also be called **micro-organisms**. You should remember from Fusion Book 1 that there are four main groups of microbe, which are **fungi**, **bacteria**, **viruses** and **protozoa**. Most microbes are harmless, but some cause diseases.

Fungi

There are many types of fungi. Some yeasts are single-celled and can only be seen through a microscope. Others, like mould, can be seen with the naked eye.

Through a microscope you can see that moulds are made of tiny threads called **hyphae**. Growing from the threads are **fruiting bodies** which make spores. Spores blow on the wind and when they fall in a suitable place a new fungus grows. Some fungi have very big fruiting bodies. The best known of these are mushrooms.

Yeasts are used in making beer, wine and bread. Many moulds are used in cheese manufacture. Many fungi, such as mushrooms, can be eaten. Some microscopic species of fungi are grown in huge tanks. The protein from them is called **mycoprotein**. It is used to make artificial meat products.

Blue cheese contains mould

There are many types of edible fungi

These 'meat' products are actually made from a fungus

Bacteria

Bacteria are just big enough to see through an ordinary light microscope. They are all single-celled. They are found in water, soil and even inside animals.

Bacteria help to decay dead animals and plants. They help to break down sewage. Some bacteria are used in making foods, such as yoghurt and cheese. They reproduce by dividing in half. This is called **binary fission**.

Bacterial cell structure

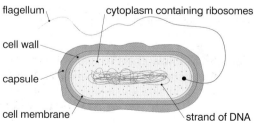

flagellum

cytoplasm containing ribosomes

cell wall

capsule

cell membrane

strand of DNA

a Make a list of some foods that use bacteria and fungi in their manufacture.

activity

Water bacteria

You may already have grown bacteria on Petri dishes containing nutrient agar jelly.

You can use this method to compare the number of bacteria in tap water and some other water.

- Put 1 cm³ of water in the middle of the nutrient agar.
- Use a sterile spreader (inoculating loop) to spread the water over the whole surface of the agar.
- Don't press too hard or you may damage the agar.
- Replace the lid and label the Petri dish. Use Sellotape to fasten the lid on the dish but do not seal. Why not?
- Repeat with the other sample of water.
- Incubate the dishes in a warm place.
- Examine the dishes after a few days but do not remove the lids. Why not?
- Describe and draw what you see? Which sample had the most bacteria? Were there any bacteria in the tap water?

Viruses

Viruses are really odd! They are the smallest microbes. They cannot grow or reproduce unless they take over the cells of another organism. For this reason many scientists do not classify them as living things! There are viruses that infect animals, plants and even bacteria.

b Why do many scientists think that viruses are not living organisms?

Not a space alien but a virus that infects bacteria!

Did You Know?

Scientists use viruses as 'tools' in some experiments!

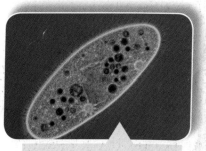

Paramecium is a protozoan

Protozoa

Protozoa are single-celled organisms. They live in ponds and damp places. Some are big enough to see with a magnifying glass.

Summary Questions

1 Make a 'mind-map' to summarise what you know about microbes. Include information about size, how they reproduce, what they look like and how they are used. After the next lesson you can add information about diseases they cause.

KEY WORDS

microbe
micro-organism
fungus
bacteria
virus
protozoan
binary fission

Microbes and Diseases

What diseases are caused by different types of microbe?

How are microbes spread from person to person?

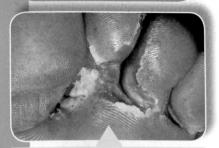

Athlete's foot is a fungal infection

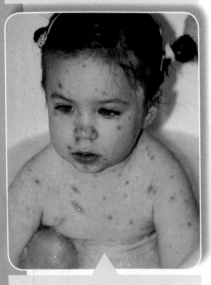

Chickenpox is caused by a virus

Help Yourself

Remember that each disease is caused by a different species of microbe. The bacteria which cause TB do not cause any other diseases. Cholera, for example, is caused by a different species of bacteria.

Some microbes can cause diseases. A disease caused by microbes is called an **infection**. Different diseases are caused by different microbes. Here are some examples:

Type of microbe	Diseases caused
Fungi	Athlete's foot, ringworm
Bacteria	Food poisoning, TB (tuberculosis), bacterial meningitis, cholera, typhoid, tetanus, impetigo
Viruses	Measles, chickenpox, common cold, flu, AIDS, viral meningitis, smallpox, rubella
Protozoa	Malaria, sleeping sickness

Microbes that cause diseases can be **transmitted** or passed from person to person. There are several different ways in which they can be transmitted:

Method of transmission	Explanation	Examples
Air	Diseases cause the patient to cough and sneeze. Tiny droplets containing the microbe are carried in the air and breathed in by someone else	Common cold, flu, whooping cough, diphtheria, tuberculosis
Food and drink	Food can be contaminated with microbes, often from faeces. Water can be contaminated with sewage	Salmonella, cholera, typhoid, dysentery
Animals	Animals, including insects, carry microbes, which are transmitted when they bite people	Rabies, malaria, sleeping sickness, yellow fever
Cuts	Bacteria in soil can infect gardeners or sports people through cuts and grazes.	Tetanus
	Microbes can be passed from person to person if they use the same needle to inject drugs	HIV, hepatitis
Contact	Microbes are passed on by touching an infected person or something they have touched such as a towel.	Impetigo, conjunctivitis, athlete's foot
	Some diseases are passed on by sexual contact	Syphilis, chlamydia, HIV
From the mother	Some microbes can be passed from mother to the fetus through the placenta	HIV, rubella

ⓐ What sort of microbe causes cholera?

ⓑ How is tuberculosis transmitted?

John Snow and cholera

John Snow was a doctor in London in the 1850s. At that time, cholera was a common disease. It causes very bad diarrhoea and vomiting, often resulting in death by dehydration. At that time we did not know about microbes and it was believed that cholera was caused by bad smells. In 1854 there was an outbreak of cholera. 500 people died. John Snow marked the deaths on a map. He noticed that most of the deaths were near a certain water pump on Broad Street. He thought the water from that pump might be the cause, so he persuaded the authorities to remove the pump handle so it could not be used.

Mosquitoes transmit malaria when they feed on blood

John Snow, the first epidemiologist

Coughs and sneezes spread diseases

Studying the spread of diseases is called **epidemiology**.

activity

Does soap remove bacteria?

- Draw a line on the bottom of a Petri dish of nutrient agar, dividing it in half.
- Label the halves 'unwashed' and 'washed'.
- Touch the 'unwashed' half of the agar jelly with your fingertips.
- Replace the lid.
- Wash your hands with soap and water and dry them with a paper towel.
- Touch the 'washed' half of the agar jelly with your fingertips.
- Use Sellotape to fasten the lid on the Petri dish but do not seal.
- Incubate the plate for a few days at 25°C.
- Describe and draw the appearance of the agar plate. Do not remove lid.
- Did washing remove all of the microbes?

Summary Questions

❶ What is meant by an 'infectious disease'?

❷ Choose a disease caused by each of the four types of microbe. Use the internet to research the disease. Make a 'fact-file' for each, giving information about how it spreads, the symptoms, treatment, etc.

❸ Imagine you are a tourist guide in London. Write a script to explain about the work of John Snow, as you walk around the Broad Street area.

KEY WORDS

infection
transmitted
epidemiology

Keeping Microbes Out

- How are microbes kept out of your body?
- How do we develop immunity to diseases?

We are surrounded by microbes. They are in the air we breathe, in our food and drink and on every surface we touch. There are microbes on our skin and in our noses, mouths and intestines. Many of these are the microbes that cause diseases. Yet it is actually quite rare for us to get an infection.

Barriers to infection
Our bodies have several ways of stopping microbes from getting in.

Keeping microbes out

Lungs
These cells have tiny hairs called cilia. Cilia move and push mucus up to your throat, where you swallow it.

These cells make mucus. Microbes and dust stick to the mucus.

Eyes

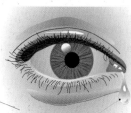

Tears contain an antiseptic. Blinking wipes the tears over your eyes.

Hair follicles

This gland makes an oily antiseptic substance.

Stomach

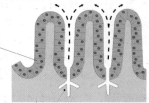

These glands make acid which kills microbes.

Cuts

Blood clots form a scab which stops microbes getting in.

Skin

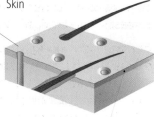

This dead layer of cells keeps microbes out.

Phagocytes engulf and destroy microbes

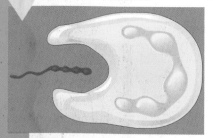

Even with these barriers, microbes sometimes get into your body. Your **immune system** provides a second line of defence. This is mainly the job of the **white blood cells**. There are two types of white blood cell:

Phagocytes surround, engulf and destroy microbes that do not belong in your body. This is called **phagocytosis**.

Lymphocytes recognise 'foreign' chemicals that do not belong in your body. These are called **antigens** and they include chemicals on the surface of microbes. Lymphocytes make **antibodies**, chemicals which stick to antigens. They make the microbes burst open or stick together in clumps. They also help phagocytes find microbes. It takes a few days to make antibodies. You might be ill during this time but when the lymphocytes start to make antibodies you will soon recover.

Each microbe has different antigens. This means a different antibody is made for each antigen.

Your white blood cells 'remember' antigens and, even better, they remember how to make antibodies against each antigen. If microbes you have had before get into your body again, you can make antibodies so quickly that the microbes are killed before you feel ill. You are immune to the disease.

ⓐ What does 'immune' mean?

Antibodies pass from a mother to a fetus through her placenta and also through breast milk. This ensures that the fetus is immune to all of the diseases its mother has had. Unfortunately these antibodies only last a few months.

Edward Jenner
In Britain in the 1700s smallpox was a serious disease, killing thousands of people each year. Edward Jenner was a country doctor in Gloucester. He heard an old country tale that said if you got cowpox, you could not get smallpox. Cowpox is a mild disease, caught from cows. In 1796 Jenner decided to investigate.

He scraped pus from a 'pock' on a milkmaid called Sarah Nelmes, who had cowpox. He spread the pus in a scratch on the arm of an eight-year-old boy called James Phipps. James got cowpox but soon recovered. Jenner then tried to give James smallpox, using pus from a smallpox patient. James did not get smallpox. The Latin word for cow is *vacca*. Jenner called his method of protecting people from diseases '**vaccination**', although now we call it **immunisation**.

Children and young people are immunised against a number of diseases by injecting **vaccine**. This contains microbes which cause a disease but have been treated to make them harmless. Your body still makes antibodies. If you are infected with the real microbes you already have the antibodies needed to destroy them.

bacteria

antibody molecule binds to antigens on the surface of the bacteria

Antibodies

activity

What immunisations have I had?

- Find out which diseases you have been immunised against.

- Find out at what age you had the immunisations.

Summary Questions

❶ Explain what is meant by:
   a) an antigen?   b) an antibody?

❷ Imagine you are a news reporter in 1796. Write the story of Jenner's discovery.

❸ Find out about the MMR vaccine and why some parents do not want their children to have it.

KEY WORDS

immune system
white blood cell
phagocyte
lymphocyte
antigen
antibody
vaccination
immunisation
vaccine

Helping the Immune System

▶▶ What are antiseptics and disinfectants?

▶▶ What are antibiotics and how were they discovered?

▶▶ How can we test the effectiveness of anti-microbial substances?

Before the 1860s the idea of microbes was unknown. Many hospital patients died following operations. At that time doctors would go from patient to patient, wearing the same clothes and without washing their hands. **Ignaz Semmelweis** was an Austrian doctor who, in 1847, observed that hand washing between examining patients reduced the death rate in a Vienna maternity hospital.

Joseph Lister was a surgeon in Edinburgh. Between 1861 and 1864 almost half of the amputation patients in his hospital died of 'sepsis'. In 1864 **Louis Pasteur** showed that decay was caused by living organisms in the air. Lister thought that sepsis could be caused by microbes. He used carbolic acid to clean wounds. He also used a **carbolic acid** spray to kill microbes in the operating theatre. This was the first example of an antiseptic.

Surgery in 1883 – the carbolic acid spray is on the right

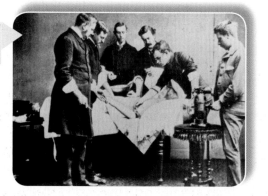

Disinfectants are chemicals that kill microbes. They are too powerful to use on living organisms as they damage cells. They are used to clean surfaces in bathrooms, kitchens, hospitals and anywhere else where there are microbes.

Antiseptics are less powerful chemicals than disinfectants. They can be used to kill microbes in cuts, grazes and in the mouth. They are too powerful to be used inside the body.

ⓐ Explain the difference between an antiseptic and a disinfectant.

Magic bullets

Doctors used antiseptics to treat infections but they often did more harm than good as they damaged living cells. Paul Ehrlich was a German scientist who had the idea of a **'magic bullet'**, a drug that would kill microbes without damaging human cells. He developed some drugs that killed microbes but also caused side effects to the patient. It was the discovery of this new type of drug that was the next big step forward.

Antibiotics

Alexander Fleming was a **bacteriologist**. One day in 1928 he was checking some agar plates with bacteria growing on them. He noticed that one of the plates had mould growing on it. He was about to throw it away when he noticed something odd. Most of the plate was covered with colonies of bacteria but the area near the mould had very few bacteria. Fleming took some of the mould and grew it on another plate with the same bacteria. He got the same result and realised that something from the mould was stopping the bacteria from growing.

Fleming wondered if this could be a way of curing diseases caused by bacteria. He identified the mould as *Penicillium notatum*. He wrote about his discovery in a **scientific journal**. Two other scientists, Howard Florey and Ernst Chain, followed up Fleming's work and eventually produced **penicillin**. It was first used on patients in 1940.

Penicillin was the first **antibiotic**, a substance made by microbes that kills bacteria without harming other organisms (such as humans). Antibiotics have no effect on viruses.

> **b** Explain how an antibiotic can be described as a 'magic bullet'.

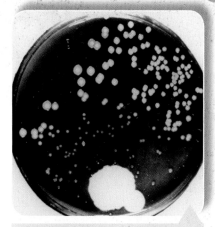

Fleming's agar plate – the mould is the large white area at the bottom

Did You Know?

Fleming, Florey and Chain were awarded the Nobel Prize for Medicine in 1945.

activity

Testing antibiotics

You will be given a Petri dish containing nutrient agar jelly.

Some bacteria have been mixed with the agar but they have not been given a chance to reproduce.

You will also be given some small paper discs, each containing an antibiotic.

- Using sterile tweezers carefully place the antibiotic discs on the agar.
- Also place a disc of plain paper on the agar.
- Make sure you take steps to avoid contamination.
- Sellotape the lid onto the Petri dish but do not seal.
- Leave the dish for a few days then observe what has happened. Do not remove the lid.
- Draw what you see.
- Did the antibiotics affect the growth of the bacteria?

Summary Questions

1. Find out what is meant by a 'scientific journal'? Why are scientific journals important?

2. Why doesn't a doctor give you antibiotics if you have flu?

3. Find out about what is meant by a broad spectrum antibiotic and a narrow spectrum antibiotic.

KEY WORDS

antiseptic
disinfectant
penicillin
antibiotic

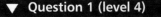

know your stuff

▼ Question 1 (level 4)

The table gives information about the nutrients in potatoes after they have been cooked in three different ways:

	Water (g)	Fat (g)	Fibre (g)	Vitamin C (mg)
100 g chips	55	7	2	8
100 g boiled, peeled potato	80	0	2	5
100 g potato baked in its skin	62	0	5	14

a Use information from the table to help you answer these:

(i) Chips are crispier than other potatoes because chips contain less of which substance? [1]

(ii) Which part of a baked potato contains most of the fibre? [1]

b How much vitamin C is there in 200 g of chips? [1]

c People do *not* always eat a balanced diet. For each fact below, choose which part of the body, from the list below, is most likely to be damaged:

heart   intestine   lung   bones

(i) Diet contains too much fat.

(ii) Diet does not have enough fibre.

(iii) Diet does not have enough calcium. [3]

▼ Question 2 (level 5)

Spots are sometimes caused by bacteria in the skin. A scientist investigated the effect of spot cream on bacteria.

a He grew bacteria on the surface of jelly in a Petri dish.

What is the best temperature to make the bacteria reproduce quickly?

Choose from the list:

−20°C   5°C   35°C   90°C   [1]

b The scientist put two small paper discs on the surface of the jelly.
One disc was soaked in spot lotion. The other disc was soaked in water.
The diagram below shows the jelly at the beginning of the experiment and two days later.

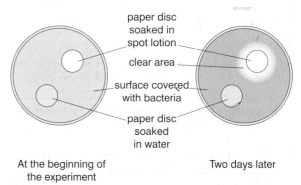

paper disc soaked in spot lotion

clear area

surface covered with bacteria

paper disc soaked in water

At the beginning of the experiment   Two days later

What was the effect of the spot cream on the bacteria? [1]

c What was the purpose of the disc soaked in water? [1]

d Give *two* safety precautions the scientist should take to avoid being harmed by the bacteria. [2]

▼ Question 3 (level 4)

a Carbon monoxide, nicotine and tar get into the lungs when a person smokes.

For each one write how it harms the body. Choose answers from the list below:

Causes lung cancer.

Is an addictive substance.

Reduces the amount of oxygen carried by red blood cells.

(i) carbon monoxide

(ii) tar

(iii) nicotine   [3]

How Science Works

▼ Question 1 (level 4)

ⓐ The graphs show the number of deaths from tuberculosis of the lungs and lung cancer, in England and Wales, between 1920 and 1960.

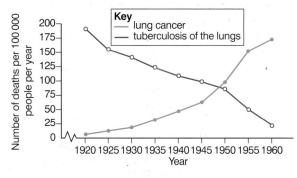

In which five-year period did the number of deaths from lung cancer rise fastest? [1]

ⓑ What treatment is given to young people today to prevent them from getting tuberculosis? [1]

▼ Question 2 (level 5)

Sailors used to suffer from an illness called 'scurvy'. Scurvy is caused by poor diet. James Lind was a doctor. He predicted that scurvy is cured by acids.

He gave six pairs of sailors with scurvy exactly the same food. He also gave each pair a dietary supplement.

Pair of sailors	Dietary supplement	Effect after one week
A	apple cider	slight recovery
B	25 drops of dilute sulfuric acid	still had scurvy
C	2 teaspoons of vinegar	still had scurvy
D	glass of sea water	still had scurvy
E	2 oranges and 1 lemon	recovered
F	herbs, spices and barley water	still had scurvy

ⓐ Does the evidence in the table support the prediction that all acids cure scurvy? Explain your answer. [1]

ⓑ (i) What was the independent variable in the investigation (the variable that Lind chose to change)? [1]

(ii) What was the dependent variable (the variable that he measured to judge the effect of changing the independent variable)? [1]

ⓒ James Lind's evidence suggested that scurvy is cured by oranges and lemons.

Other scientists knew that oranges and lemons contained citric acid. They predicted that citric acid would cure scurvy but when they tried it, it did not work.

Make a new prediction that fits the evidence. [1]

ⓓ Explain why James Lind should have carried out his investigation for longer than one week. [1]

▼ Question 3 (level 7)

ⓐ In 1967 an immunisation programme against measles began. Children were injected with measles vaccine. This made them immune to the disease.

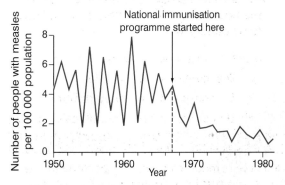

The graph shows how the number of people with measles varied between 1950 and 1980.

(i) What is meant by 'immune'? [1]

(ii) When a person is given the measles vaccine they produce a substance that kills the measles virus. What is the name of this type of substance? [1]

Variation and Genetics

The Natural History Museum

Sorting and identifying

The girl in the photo is in the Natural History Museum in London. She is using the internet to find out more information about the animals she is studying.

Exhibitions of animals and plants at the museum are displayed according to the ways in which scientists sort them into groups.

How do we sort animals?

Carlo and Jo have a collection of animal pictures. They decide to sort them into groups to display them.

Carlo and Jo's display

a How have Carlo and Jo decided how to sort the animals into groups?

Sorting animals into groups

- Look at the way Carlo and Jo have sorted their animal pictures.
- Where would you put the picture of the duck?
- Working with a partner, decide on two other ways to sort the animals into groups.
- Are there any animals that do not fit easily into one group? Why?
- Make a poster to show how you sort the animals.

Fingerprints

Forensic scientists can identify people by looking at their fingerprints. Everyone's fingerprints are unique. Yet all fingerprints belong to one of three basic types:

Once a fingerprint has been classified as a loop, an arch or a whorl then we can sort it into one of several sub-groups. This makes it easier to match a fingerprint found at a crime scene with those kept on record. In a similar way, scientists sort living organisms into groups then subdivide them into subgroups, etc.

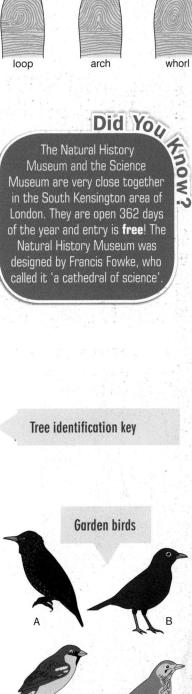

Fingerprint types

loop   arch   whorl

Did You Know?

The Natural History Museum and the Science Museum are very close together in the South Kensington area of London. They are open 362 days of the year and entry is **free**! The Natural History Museum was designed by Francis Fowke, who called it 'a cathedral of science'.

Identification keys

Scientists often use keys to help identify animals and plants. A key has a number of questions or statements. Start at the beginning and the key will lead you to the animal or plant you want to identify. There are two types of key:

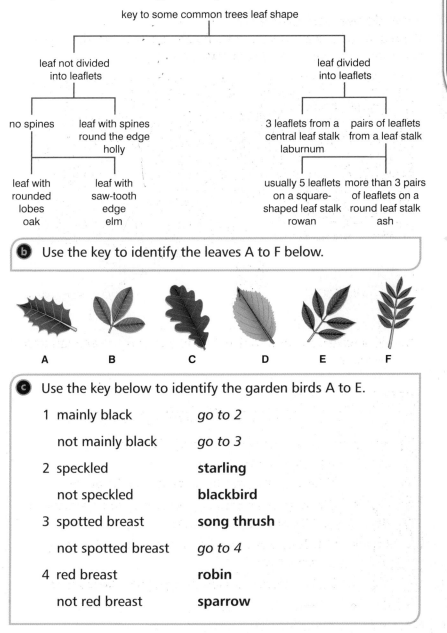

key to some common trees leaf shape

leaf not divided into leaflets

leaf divided into leaflets

no spines

leaf with spines round the edge
holly

3 leaflets from a central leaf stalk
laburnum

pairs of leaflets from a leaf stalk

leaf with rounded lobes
oak

leaf with saw-tooth edge
elm

usually 5 leaflets on a square-shaped leaf stalk
rowan

more than 3 pairs of leaflets on a round leaf stalk
ash

Tree identification key

b Use the key to identify the leaves A to F below.

A   B   C   D   E   F

Garden birds

c Use the key below to identify the garden birds A to E.

1	mainly black	*go to 2*
	not mainly black	*go to 3*
2	speckled	**starling**
	not speckled	**blackbird**
3	spotted breast	**song thrush**
	not spotted breast	*go to 4*
4	red breast	**robin**
	not red breast	**sparrow**

A   B   C   D   E

Putting Living Things into Groups

- ▶▶ What is meant by the terms 'species' and 'hybrid'?
- ▶▶ How are living things put into groups?
- ▶▶ How can the groups be sub-divided?

Classification

Scientists have identified millions of species of living organisms and they are constantly finding new ones. If a scientist collects an organism it will be carefully observed and described. It is then compared with known **species**. If it does not match a known organism then it will be classified as a new species.

Scientists use a system called **taxonomic classification**, which was first invented by **Carolus Linnaeus** in 1735. He looked at thousands of plants and animals and gave each one a Latin name. For example, humans have the Latin name *Homo sapiens*. We always write the Latin name of a species in *italics* (or underline it if it is handwritten). The first name is always written with a capital letter and the second name with a small letter.

The two main species of rat are the black rat and the brown rat (which is sometimes called the Norway rat, even though it probably came from China) but there are many other animals, also called rats such as 'water rats' and 'kangaroo rats', which are not really rats. In Spanish a rat is called 'rata', while in German it is 'Ratte'. Say *Rattus rattus* to a science expert anywhere in the world and they will know what you mean. It is the Latin name of the black rat, while *Rattus norvegicus* is the brown rat.

Black rat

Brown rat

ⓐ What is *Homo sapiens*?

ⓑ What is the difference between *Rattus rattus* and *Rattus norvegicus*?

What is a species?

Members of the same species can breed with each other and produce **fertile** offspring. A labrador and a poodle can breed with each other because they are both dogs. Some animals of different, but closely related species, can breed together to produce a **hybrid**. A male lion and a female tiger produce a hybrid called a **liger**.

A male donkey and female horse produce a hybrid called a **mule**. Both of these hybrids are unable to reproduce. That means the lion and tiger, and the horse and donkey, are each separate species.

A liger is a hybrid of a male lion and a female tiger

Sorting into groups

Living things are sorted into five main groups called **kingdoms**:

Monera – the bacteria and their relatives

Protoctist – organisms with just one cell, such as paramecium

The five kingdoms

Fungi – moulds, mushrooms and their relatives

Animals – organisms that move about and have a nervous system

Plants – organisms that make food by photosynthesis

Each kingdom is then divided into smaller groups depending on the features they share. Organisms in the same group have similar features because they evolved from common ancestors. If a new species is discovered it is usually fitted into an existing group. Sometimes a new species is so different it is given a whole new group.

activity

Sorting and describing

Find out about one example from each of the five kingdoms. Draw a picture or find a photograph of each one. Use these to make a display that clearly shows the differences between each kingdom.

Summary Questions

1. Find out what these animals are:
   a) *Panthera leo*   b) *Panthera tigris*   c) *Felis silvestris*

2. What does *Homo sapiens* actually mean?

3. How do we know that lions and tigers are different species?

4. A 'zonkey' is a hybrid, but what are its parents? What other hybrid animals are known?

KEY WORDS

species
taxanomic classification
hybrid
kingdom

Vertebrates

> ▶▶ What do we mean by a vertebrate?
>
> ▶▶ What are the vertebrate groups and how are animals grouped in them?

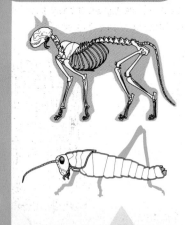

The cat is a vertebrate with a skeleton inside its body. The locust is an invertebrate with an exoskeleton outside its body, shown in green

Backbone or no backbone?

We can divide the animal kingdom into two groups:

- **vertebrates**, which have a backbone
- **invertebrates**, which do not have a backbone.

Vertebrates have certain characteristics in common:

- a central nervous system, protected by the backbone
- a head
- a body which is symmetrical from side to side
- an internal skeleton made of bone or cartilage.

Fish

- live in water
- lay eggs in water
- swim using fins
- breathe through gills
- have moist, scaly skin.

Amphibians

- can live on land
- lay jelly-covered eggs in water
- have four legs
- have lungs and absorb oxygen through their skin
- have moist skin without scales.

Reptiles

- lay eggs with soft, leathery shells
- breathe through lungs
- have dry, scaly skin.

Birds

- lay eggs with hard shells
- have two legs and two wings
- breathe through lungs
- have feathers
- maintain a warm body temperature (warm blooded).

Mammals

- give birth to live babies and make milk to feed them
- breathe through lungs
- have fur or hair
- have external ears
- maintain a warm body temperature (warm blooded).

Did You Know?

Only about 5% of animals are vertebrates. 95% of animals are invertebrates.

a What feature do all vertebrates have?

b What are the similarities between birds and mammals?
How are they different?

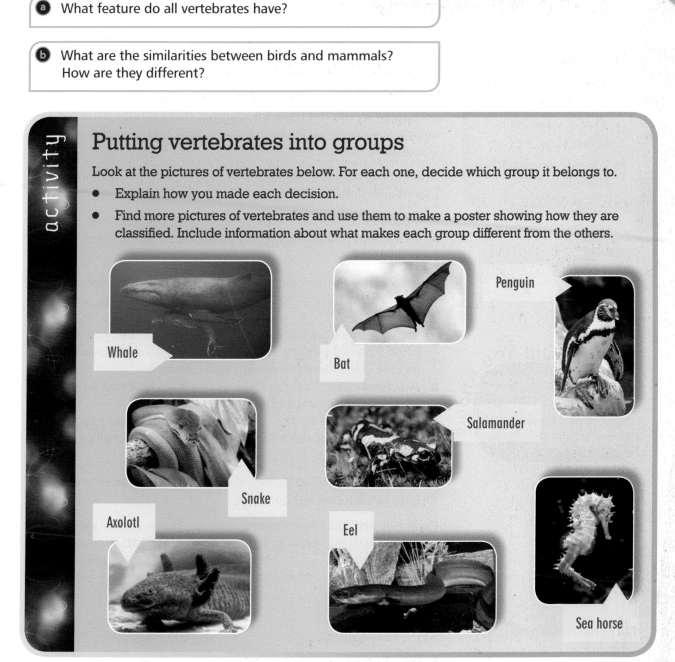

activity

Putting vertebrates into groups

Look at the pictures of vertebrates below. For each one, decide which group it belongs to.

- Explain how you made each decision.
- Find more pictures of vertebrates and use them to make a poster showing how they are classified. Include information about what makes each group different from the others.

Whale

Bat

Penguin

Snake

Salamander

Axolotl

Eel

Sea horse

Summary Questions

1 What group do humans belong to? Explain your answer.

2 What features are the same in birds and reptiles? What features are different?

3 Why are reptiles better adapted to live on land?

4 Find out about the platypus. What makes it a very odd mammal? Why is it classified as a mammal?

?

Invertebrates

▶▶ What are invertebrates and what are their main features?

▶▶ How are they sorted into groups?

Earthworm

Did You Know?

The word 'millipede' means 1000 legs (feet), but most species have between 80 and 400 legs and the most for any species is 750. That's still a lot of legs!

Invertebrate groups

Most of the animals in the world are **invertebrates**. These are animals which do not have a backbone. There is huge variation among the invertebrates, which are divided into several groups. The groups include:

Annelids which have round bodies, divided into many segments. Examples include earthworms.

Arthropods have a hard external skeleton, a body divided into segments and jointed legs. The arthropods are sub-divided into four groups:

- **Insects** have three pairs of legs and a body in three segments. They usually have wings. Examples include flies, bees, ants and butterflies.
- **Crustaceans** have between five and seven pairs of legs and often a pair of pincers. They have a very hard shell. Examples include crabs, lobsters, prawns and woodlice.
- **Arachnids** have four pairs of legs and a body in two segments. They include spiders and scorpions.
- **Myriapods** have bodies which are divided into many segments. They have legs on each segment. Centipedes and millipedes are myriapods.

Cnidarians have round bodies, surrounded by tentacles and include jellyfish and sea anemones.

Echinoderms' bodies are arranged in five parts around a circle. They have spiny skin and tiny tube-like feet. Starfish and sea urchins are echinoderms.

Jellyfish

Starfish

This tapeworm from a cow is several metres long!

Flatworms have flat bodies made of many segments. Many of them are parasites, like tapeworms, which live in the guts of other animals.

Molluscs often have a protective shell. Many types of mollusc, such as slugs and snails, move on a single foot. Bivalves, such as mussels, protect themselves in a pair of shells. The **cephalopods**, such as the octopus and squid, are the most advanced invertebrates and like molluscs have a circulatory system.

Octopus

Roundworms have long, thin worm-like bodies, without segments. Many roundworms are parasites.

Sponges could easily be mistaken for plants, but they do not photosynthesise and lack cell walls.

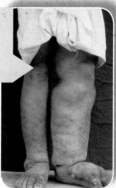

Elephantiasis is caused by a parasitic roundworm

> **ⓐ** In what ways are a spider and a fly the same? How do they differ?

> **ⓑ** Why do we classify sponges as animals and not plants?

Classifying invertebrates

Branching diagrams and **Venn diagrams** are useful for helping to classify organisms. They can be used to show the **hierarchical** nature of classification – how organisms are sorted into smaller and smaller groups:

Stove-pipe sponge

Invertebrates
├── Annelids
├── Sponges
├── Arthropods
│   ├── Insects
│   ├── Crustaceans
│   ├── Arachnids
│   └── Myriapods
├── Cnidarians
├── Echindermus
├── Flatworms
├── Molluscs
└── Roundworms

Branching diagram

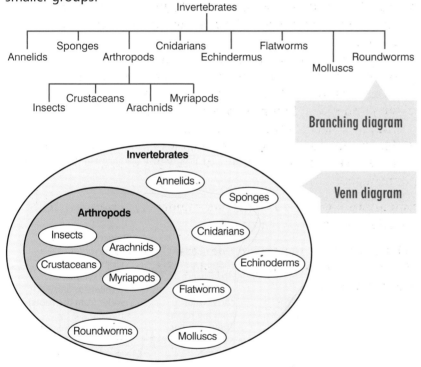

Venn diagram

Invertebrates, Annelids, Sponges, Arthropods (Insects, Arachnids, Crustaceans, Myriapods), Cnidarians, Echinoderms, Flatworms, Roundworms, Molluscs

activity

Classifying invertebrates

Use books and the internet to find pictures of different invertebrates. Use either a branching diagram or a Venn diagram to make a presentation about classification of invertebrates. Make sure you include information about how they are sorted into groups.

Summary Questions

❶ Which arthropod group has:
  a) 6 legs?   b) 8 legs?   c) more than 20 legs?

❷ Slugs are different from many other members of their group. How are they different?

❸ Which is the odd one out and why?
  a) earthworm, slug, snail, squid
  b) butterfly, wasp, spider, ladybird
  c) crab, centipede, scorpion, starfish

KEY WORDS

invertebrate
branching diagram
Venn diagram

Plants

Sorting plants into groups

In the past, fungi were classified as plants but they have now been given a kingdom of their own. Some microscopic green organisms were also classified as plants but they are now placed among the protoctists and monera.

The plant kingdom includes all multicellular organisms with cell walls made of **cellulose**. Plants use light energy to make their own food from carbon dioxide and water in the process of **photosynthesis**.

✚ Help Yourself

Write a word equation and a symbol equation for the process of photosynthesis.

Classifying plants

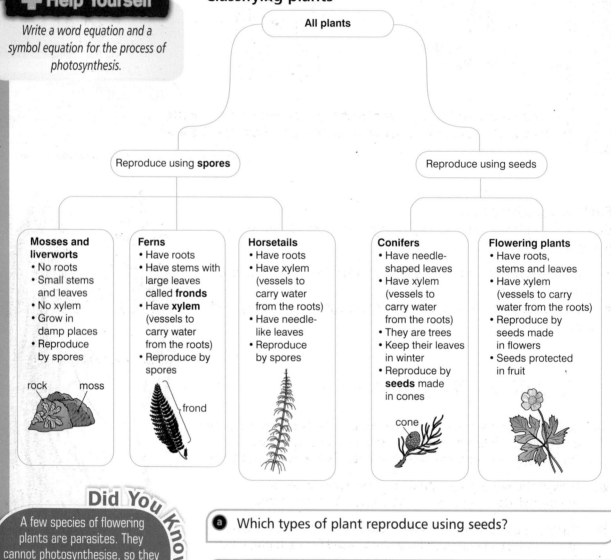

All plants

Reproduce using **spores**   Reproduce using seeds

Mosses and liverworts
• No roots
• Small stems and leaves
• No xylem
• Grow in damp places
• Reproduce by spores

rock   moss

Ferns
• Have roots
• Have stems with large leaves called **fronds**
• Have **xylem** (vessels to carry water from the roots)
• Reproduce by spores

frond

Horsetails
• Have roots
• Have xylem (vessels to carry water from the roots)
• Have needle-like leaves
• Reproduce by spores

Conifers
• Have needle-shaped leaves
• Have xylem (vessels to carry water from the roots)
• They are trees
• Keep their leaves in winter
• Reproduce by **seeds** made in cones

cone

Flowering plants
• Have roots, stems and leaves
• Have xylem (vessels to carry water from the roots)
• Reproduce by seeds made in flowers
• Seeds protected in fruit

Did You Know?

A few species of flowering plants are parasites. They cannot photosynthesise, so they grow roots into another plant to take food from its tissues.

ⓐ Which types of plant reproduce using seeds?

ⓑ Which types of plant grow roots?

activity

Classifying plants

Look at the photographs of some plants. Decide which group each one fits into.

A

B

C

D

E

F

G

Your teacher will give you some more plant specimens to classify.
Make a display or presentation to explain how plants are classified.

Further classification

Like animals, plant groups can be further sub-divided. Flowering plants are divided into two groups:

- **monocotyledons** which have long pointed leaves with parallel veins
- **dicotyledons** which have broader leaves with veins that spread out.

Dicotyledon and monocotyledon

Summary Questions

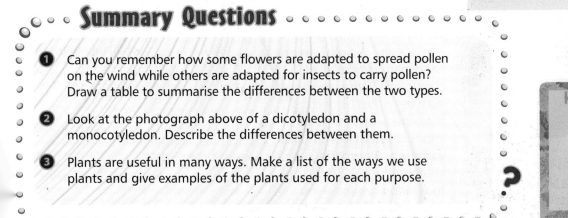

1. Can you remember how some flowers are adapted to spread pollen on the wind while others are adapted for insects to carry pollen? Draw a table to summarise the differences between the two types.

2. Look at the photograph above of a dicotyledon and a monocotyledon. Describe the differences between them.

3. Plants are useful in many ways. Make a list of the ways we use plants and give examples of the plants used for each purpose.

KEY WORDS

spore
xylem
seed
monocotyledon
dicotyledon

Variation

- Why do we look similar, but not identical, to our parents?
- What do we mean by inherited and environmental variation?
- What is continuous and discontinuous variation?

Great Debates

Is intelligence inherited? Is it environmental? Is it a combination of both? How could you find out in humans?

The shape of this tree has been permanently affected by growing in a windy environment

Hydrangea flowers vary in colour depending on the pH of the soil – blue flowers mean acid soil and pink flowers mean alkaline soil

Spot the difference

Family

You wouldn't be likely to mistake a human for an animal of another species. Humans have many similarities. We can all recognise our friends and family as individuals, however, as all humans are different. Differences between members of the same species are called **variation**.

We mostly look similar to other members of our family but (unless we are identical twins) people can still tell us apart.

a Make a list of similarities between the people in the photograph.

b Make a list of differences between them.

Inherited and environmental variation

Many of the features you listed, such as eye colour, hair colour and the shape of your ears, are **inherited** characteristics. This means they are passed on to us from our parents.

Some features, such as scars, are not inherited. We call these **environmental** characteristics.

Many characteristics are a combination of inheritance *and* environment. Tall parents are very likely to give their children the **potential** to grow tall. If the children have a poor diet, however, they may not reach their potential.

c Which of this woman's features are inherited variation? Which features are environmental variation?

Discontinuous and continuous variation

We differ from each other in many ways – height, weight, handspan, gender, eye colour, etc. Some variation, such as gender, is one or the other – male or female. This is called **discontinuous variation**. Blood group is another example. There are four blood groups – you cannot be in-between blood groups.

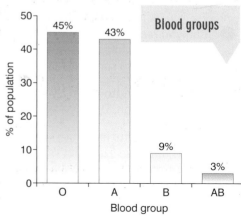

Blood groups

% of population / Blood group

- O — 45%
- A — 43%
- B — 9%
- AB — 3%

Other variation is not clear cut. A pupil in Year 9 could be any height between, say, 130 and 190 cm. This is an example of **continuous variation**.

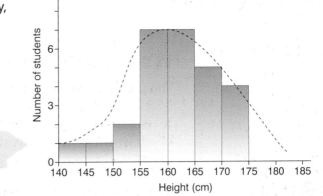

Heights of Year 9 girls

Measuring variation

Investigate the range of variation of pupils in your class. Make measurements and observations of features such as:

- height
- hair colour
- eye colour
- body temperature
- male or female
- handspan
- tongue rolling – ask people to roll their tongue as shown in the drawing.

Measuring handspan

Tongue rolling

Record your data in a table or spreadsheet. Use your data to produce graphs showing the range of variation for each feature. For some characteristics, such as height, you may find it more useful to record each person within a range, for example 146–149.9 cm, 150–154.9 cm etc.

- Explain how you chose to display your data.
- Describe the patterns shown by your data.
- Georgina suggests that it would be better to measure all of the pupils in Year 9. Do you agree? Explain your answer.
- Rachel says they should measure everyone in the school. Apart from the resulting disruption, what other problems could this cause?

Summary Questions

1. Make a list of ways in which people show variation. Sort them into inherited, environmental or a combination of both.

2. Look at your list in question 1. For each example, say if it is continuous or discontinuous.

KEY WORDS

variation
inherited
environmental
discontinuous variation
continuous variation

Genes and Inheritance

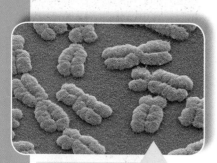

Human chromosomes

It's in your genes

You already know that the nucleus of every cell in your body contains a set of **genes**. These contain all of the genetic information needed to make you. Each gene has information needed to control the development of a characteristic, such as eye colour or hair colour.

Genes are carried on pairs of **chromosomes** in the cell nucleus. Human cell nuclei have 46 chromosomes in 23 pairs. Different species have different numbers of chromosomes (but it is always an even number).

ⓐ Why do organisms always have an even number of chromosomes?

When cells divide to make new body cells they make an exact copy of all of the chromosomes. When human eggs and sperm are made, however, they only contain half a set of chromosomes: 23 chromosomes instead of 46.

When an egg is fertilised by a sperm, the chromosomes carried by the egg pair up with the chromosomes carried by the sperm. In humans, the egg's 23 chromosomes join up with the sperm's 23 chromosomes to make 46 chromosomes again, with a mixture of its parents' genes. Each chromosome in a pair has a copy of each gene. So each cell contains two copies of each gene – one from the mother and one from the father.

ⓑ Where are the gametes in flowering plants?

As the fertilised egg divides to form an embryo, exact copies of its chromosomes are made each time.

parent cell
3 pairs of chromosomes

pairs of chromosomes separate

chromosomes pass into sperm or eggs

sperm cells have half the number of chromosomes of a body cell

How sperms are made in an animal with 3 pairs of chromosomes

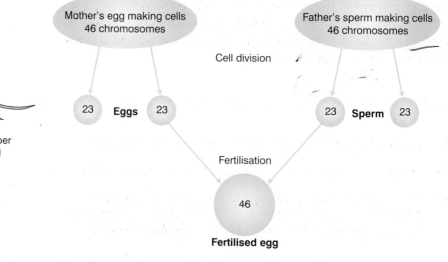

Mother's egg making cells
46 chromosomes

Father's sperm making cells
46 chromosomes

Cell division

23 **Eggs** 23

23 **Sperm** 23

Fertilisation

46

Fertilised egg

Brothers' and sisters' genes come from the same parents, so why aren't they the same? When gametes are made, each one is unique because the different genes on each chromosome get jumbled up. Imagine a very simple organism with one pair of chromosomes made up of just five genes:

Did You Know?

Chromosomes are made of a chemical called 'deoxyribonucleic acid'. Luckily we normally just call it DNA!
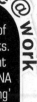

PARENT'S GENES

GAMETE'S GENES

The parent has ten genes arranged in two sets.

Here are four different combinations of five genes in the gamete. How many more are there?

science@work

Everyone (except identical twins) inherits a different set of genes from each of their parents. This means we all have different DNA. Forensic scientists use DNA profiling or 'genetic fingerprinting' to identify people from small traces of tissue such as blood, saliva or semen, left at a crime scene.

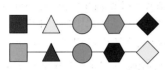

Parent's genes can be combined in many ways

So what about identical twins?

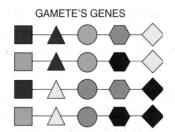

Identical twins

But my teacher says my jeans come from my parents!

Identical twins have exactly the same genes. What does this tell us about the egg and sperm they came from?

Identical twins happen when one sperm fertilises one egg. The fertilised egg starts to divide as normal but then splits into two parts, each of which grows into a separate baby, with the same genes as its twin.

Non-identical twins are formed when a woman releases two eggs at the same time which are then fertilised by two separate sperms. Non-identical twins are the same as normal brothers and sisters except they are born at the same time.

Summary Questions

1. Where are chromosomes found? What are they made of?

2. How are the chromosomes in a gamete different from other cells?

3. Find out about DNA profiling. Make a poster or computer presentation explaining how it works. What precautions must forensic scientists take when collecting samples of tissue?

KEY WORDS

gene
chromosome
gamete

Passing on the Genes

Our inheritance

We have 23 pairs of chromosomes. One pair of chromosomes, called the X and Y chromosomes, decides your sex. Girls have two X chromosomes, while boys have an X chromosome and a Y chromosome.

Women can only pass on X chromosomes in their eggs. Men can pass on an X chromosome or a Y chromosome in their sperm. Half of a man's sperm carry an X chromosome and half carry a Y chromosome.

> **a** Why are there no babies with two Y chromosomes?

Inheriting eye colour

You have two copies of the gene for each inherited characteristic – one from your mother and one for your father. Let us look at eye colour. Different versions of genes are called **alleles**. If you have two blue alleles then it's easy – you have blue eyes. Likewise, if you have two brown alleles you have brown eyes. But what if you have one blue-eyed allele and one brown-eyed allele? Do you get one blue eye and one brown eye?

The brown allele is **dominant**. It is 'stronger' than a blue allele, which is **recessive**. So if you have a brown allele and a blue allele you have brown eyes! If you have two alleles the same, you are described as **homozygous** for the characteristic. If you have different alleles you are **heterozygous**.

* What decides whether we are male or female?
* How do we inherit particular features?
* What can we learn by looking at family trees?

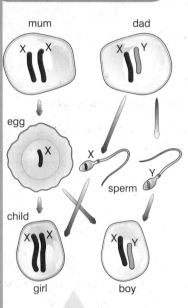

How your sex is decided

Inheriting eye colour

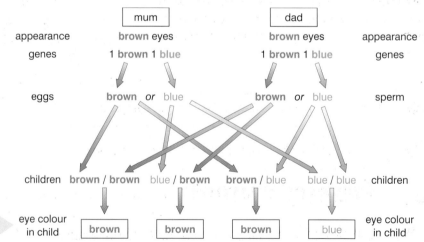

The diagram shows the possible outcomes if two people who both have one brown and one blue allele have a baby. They have a 1 in 4 chance of having a baby with blue eyes and a 3 in 4 chance of having a baby with brown eyes.

Punnet squares

Punnet squares are special charts used to show possible combinations of genes, based on the genes of the parents.

We can use symbols to represent different alleles. **B** stands for a dominant brown-eye allele and **b** stands for a recessive blue-eye allele.

The mum and dad in the second diagram opposite are both shown as **Bb** (they are heterozygous).

We can use a Punnet square to work out the possible outcomes. The information from the diagram is shown in the Punnet square below:

		Mother brown eyes	
	alleles	B	b
Father brown eyes	B	BB brown	Bb brown
	b	Bb brown	bb blue

Each child the parents have has a ¾ chance of brown eyes and ¼ chance of blue eyes.

Use Punnet squares to work out the chance of having brown or blue eyes of the children of the following parents:

- Russ has the alleles BB. Fatima has the alleles bb.
- Charlie has the alleles Bb. Rachel has the alleles bb.
- Freddie has the alleles BB. Rebecca has the alleles Bb.

Family trees

The Morgan family all have red hair. Red hair is recessive to brown hair. The family tree shows the hair colour of the Morgan and Jones families.

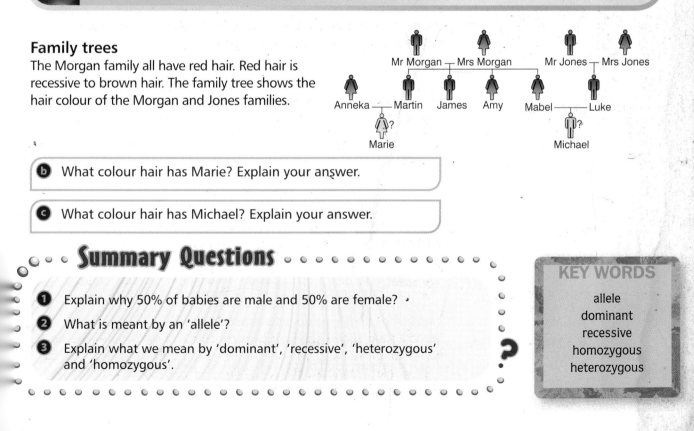

b What colour hair has Marie? Explain your answer.

c What colour hair has Michael? Explain your answer.

Summary Questions

1 Explain why 50% of babies are male and 50% are female?

2 What is meant by an 'allele'?

3 Explain what we mean by 'dominant', 'recessive', 'heterozygous' and 'homozygous'.

KEY WORDS

allele
dominant
recessive
homozygous
heterozygous

Breeding Animals

> ▸▸ What characteristics are required in domestic animals?
>
> ▸▸ How can selective breeding produce animals with the required characteristics?
>
> ▸▸ Do you think that selective breeding is ethical?

One man and his dog

There are many breeds of dogs, which come in many shapes and sizes. We use some dogs as working dogs.

Sled dogs have to be strong, with good stamina

Guide dogs need to be intelligent and calm

a Think of some more examples of working dogs.

activity

Working dogs

Dogs have characteristics that make them suited for a particular purpose.

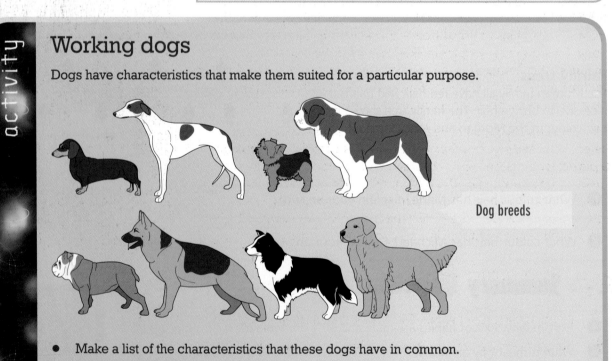

Dog breeds

- Make a list of the characteristics that these dogs have in common.
- Make a list of features that are different in each breed.
- Use the internet to find out what each dog is (or was) used for. Describe what features make it suitable for that job.

So, you're a working dog, are you?

Although dog breeds look quite different, they all belong to the same species. Over thousands of years they have been bred from wolves, *Canis lupus*. Domestic dogs are a sub-species of wolves. This means that they are different from wolves. Dogs do not normally breed with wolves but it is possible. Dogs are given the name *Canis lupus familiaris*.

b How do we know that all breeds of dog are members of the same species?

c What is meant by a sub-species?

Selective breeding

Dachshunds were bred to hunt badgers. They have to be thin and flexible to fit into a badger's **sett**. Breeders would always **select** the most suitable dogs to breed from – those with the longest, thinnest body. Their puppies were more likely to inherit these desirable characteristics. Puppies which were not suitable would not be selected for breeding. Over several generations the desired characteristics became more exaggerated, producing a separate breed of dog.

Many species of animal have been domesticated and, through **selective breeding**, developed into animals especially suitable for a particular purpose. Selective breeding has produced cattle that make more milk or milk of a high quality. Others produce lots of meat without too much fat. Other desirable characteristics are resistance to disease, ease of giving birth and even udders which are a good shape to fit milking machines!

Summary Questions

1 What characteristics would farmers look for in sheep?

2 Draw a flow chart to summarise the process of selective breeding.

3 Find out about health issues that affect some breeds of dog which are caused by selective breeding of some 'desirable' characteristics.

KEY WORDS

selective breeding
unethical

Selective Breeding in Plants

> ▸▸ What characteristics are selected for breeding in plants?
>
> ▸▸ How is selective breeding carried out in plants?

An 'ear' of wheat

Selecting food crops

Cereals such as rice, wheat, maize, oats and barley are probably the most important food crops in the world. A good source of carbohydrate, protein and fibre, they are a major source of energy for people and farm animals worldwide. It might surprise you to know that when you are eating bread, pasta, rice or sweet corn you are actually eating grass seeds!

People collected grass seeds as a food source thousands of years ago. Then they started sowing seeds they had harvested and saved the previous year. By sowing the biggest and best seeds, they selected the 'best' genes. Gradually small grass plants became the cereal crops, with lots of large seeds, which we know today.

The results of selective breeding in plants are known as **varieties** rather than breeds.

> **a** Apart from lots of large seeds, what other features are desirable in a cereal crop?

Another plant which has produced a number of food crops is the Brassica. Selective breeding, over hundreds of years, has developed varieties that use different parts of the plant as food:

- leaves – cabbage (of which there are many varieties) and greens
- buds – Brussels sprouts
- flowers – cauliflower and broccoli
- stem – kohlrabi

There's even a variety with long straight stems that is used for making walking sticks and another grown for its ornamental leaves!

Did You Know?

A 2002 survey identified Brussel sprouts as the vegetable most hated by British schoolchildren!

A red cabbage variety

Kohlrabi

Ornamental cabbage

Hand pollination

Plant breeders select two varieties of plant that have desirable characteristics. For example, a tomato plant with good flavour tomatoes could be crossed with a plant that produces bigger than average fruit. The breeder will use a brush to collect pollen from the anthers of one plant and transfer it to the stigmas of the other. The anthers are removed from the plant that receives the pollen so it cannot self-pollinate.

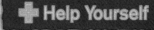
Help Yourself

Pollination is the movement of pollen from the male anther of one flower to the female stigma of another flower. *Fertilisation* is where a tube grows from a pollen grain and the pollen nucleus moves down it to fuse with the ovule nucleus.

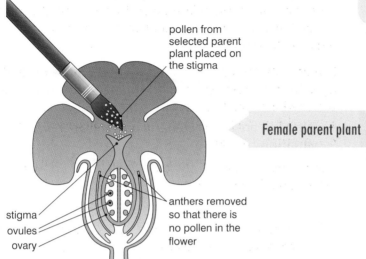

pollen from selected parent plant placed on the stigma

Female parent plant

stigma
ovules
ovary

anthers removed so that there is no pollen in the flower

The plant is then kept in a place where insects cannot transfer more pollen from elsewhere. The seeds are collected and grown to produce a new generation. Any plants showing the desired characteristics are then bred together and the process repeated for several generations until the desired plant is produced.

Summary Questions

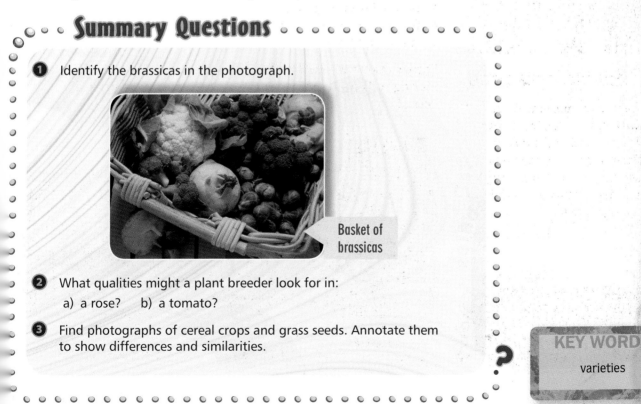

❶ Identify the brassicas in the photograph.

Basket of brassicas

❷ What qualities might a plant breeder look for in:
a) a rose? b) a tomato?

❸ Find photographs of cereal crops and grass seeds. Annotate them to show differences and similarities.

KEY WORDS

varieties

Evolution

Charles Darwin

Scientists used to believe that all living things had been the same since the Earth was created.

Charles Darwin was a scientist on board *HMS Beagle*, which sailed around the world from 1831 to 1836. In 1835 he was in the Galapagos Islands, off the Pacific coast of South America. He studied **finches**, which lived on the islands. He noticed that different finches had different beaks, which matched their different diets.

Darwin noted two important facts:

- Offspring are slightly different from their parents; this is called **variation**.
- Characteristics **inherited** from parents are passed on to the next generation.

Darwin thought that seed eating finches reached the Galapagos islands from South America. There wasn't much food so the finches had to **compete** for food. Finches with different shaped beaks were able to eat other foods so they were more likely to survive. The finches that were most suited to their environment survived and passed on their genes. Darwin called this **natural selection**. Natural selection is the process which causes **evolution**.

Darwin spent 20 years working on his ideas which he published in a book called *'On the Origin of Species by means of Natural Selection'* in 1859. Even after it was published, it took many years before his ideas were accepted by most people.

▸▸ Who was Charles Darwin and what did he do?

▸▸ What is meant by the term 'evolution'?

▸▸ How did giraffes evolve?

▸▸ How can we use evidence to support or disprove a theory?

Did You Know?

On 24 June 2006 a tortoise named Harriet died, aged 176, in an Australian zoo. It is claimed that Harriet was collected in the Galapagos Islands in 1835 by Charles Darwin. Harriet may actually have met Charles Darwin, who died in 1892!

Great Debates

Some people believe that the Earth was created in six days, as described in the Bible. Some believe that the Theory of Evolution should not be taught in schools, or that at least the Creationist view should be given equal importance. What do you think? Make sure you can use evidence to support your views.

Darwin's finches show six different beak types

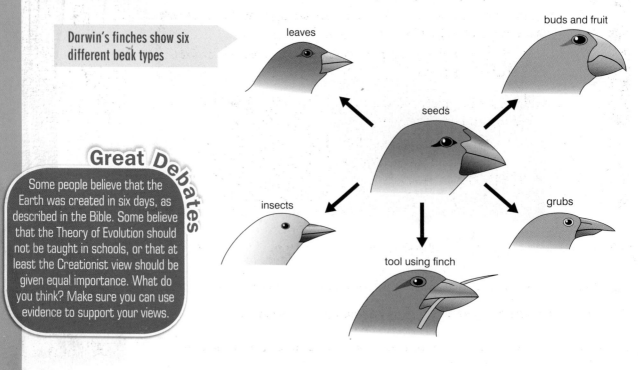

leaves

buds and fruit

seeds

insects

grubs

tool using finch

One species of finch even developed the ability to use thorns to get insects from tree bark!

> **a** Where are the Galapagos Islands?

Evolving giraffes

In every population there is variation – some animals were taller than others.

Some giraffes can reach the top of the tree. They get more food and are healthier than shorter giraffes.

These survivors are likely to have more babies. They will pass on their useful genes to their offspring who will also show this beneficial variation.

Evidence for evolution

Scientific theories are based on **evidence**.

Fossil remains of extinct animals show that they have not always been the same. They show links between extinct species and those living now.

Anatomy – many animals have similar structures because they evolved from a common ancestor. For example, many mammals have a five-fingered limb (human hand, whale flipper, bat wing).

DNA from closely related species is quite similar, while other species have more differences in their DNA.

activity

Learning from fossils

A fossil of Archaeopteryx

The photograph shows a fossil of Archaeopteryx, an evolutionary link between reptiles and birds.

- Describe Archaeopteryx and say which features are like a bird and which are like a reptile.

The drawing is an artist's impression, based on the fossil of Archaeopteryx.

- Describe the features that the artist has based on evidence and those which are guesswork.

An artist's impression of Archaeopteryx

Summary Questions

1 Explain what we mean by: a) natural selection   b) evolution.

2 Why did it take many years for Darwin's theory to be accepted?

KEY WORDS

variation
inherited
natural selection
evolution

Cloning and Gene Therapy

- ▶▶ What is a clone?
- ▶▶ How can cloning be carried out?
- ▶▶ What is gene therapy?
- ▶▶ Is it ethical to clone humans?

➕ Help Yourself

You learned about asexual reproduction in plants in Fusion Book 1. When plants reproduce by runners, bulbs and tubers the results are clones of the parent plant.

activity

Cuttings

- Get a geranium plant.
- Cut off a stem just below where a leaf joins.
- Remove the lower leaves so there are two or three leaves on the plant.
- Dip the cut end in rooting powder. This helps the stem to make roots.
- Put the cutting in compost.
- Cover the pot with a polythene bag. This keeps the plant moist. After two or three weeks it will grow roots.

⚠ **Safety:** Take care if using a scalpel.

Attack of the clones!

This sounds like something out of science fiction. Clones are some sort of bad guy aliens, killing people with ray guns, aren't they? The truth is a lot less frightening. Potatoes are clones and they aren't very scary!

Take me to your larder!

Clones are organisms that have identical genes. Many plants make clones naturally (as do a few animals). Spider plants reproduce by growing runners. Each runner has a little 'plantlet' at the end. When these touch the ground they grow roots. Eventually the runner withers away and a new plant is formed. This new plant is genetically identical to the parent.

> **ⓐ** Explain why identical twins are clones.

Cloning mammals

Dolly the sheep was the first cloned mammal. She was cloned in 1996 by scientists at Edinburgh University.

Cloning does not always work. Dolly was born after 276 previous attempts. In 2003 Dolly was put down after she was found to be suffering from arthritis and lung disease. These conditions are unusual in a sheep of Dolly's age and some scientists think that she was suffering from premature ageing.

Since Dolly, many other mammals have been cloned. There are various reasons for cloning animals including:

- Much loved **pets** which have died and been replaced with a clone.
- **Endangered species** which are in danger of becoming extinct.
- Making exact copies of **high quality animals** for breeding.
- A rich Russian has offered a cash prize to anyone who uses DNA from a **mammoth** found frozen in permafrost.
- Cloning humans to **grow organs** for transplants.

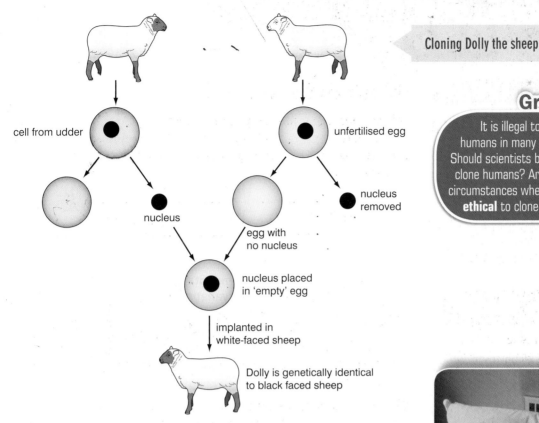

Cloning Dolly the sheep

cell from udder

unfertilised egg

nucleus removed

nucleus

egg with no nucleus

nucleus placed in 'empty' egg

implanted in white-faced sheep

Dolly is genetically identical to black faced sheep

Great Debates

It is illegal to clone humans in many countries. Should scientists be allowed to clone humans? Are there any circumstances when it might be **ethical** to clone humans?

Gene therapy

The boy in the photograph has **cystic fibrosis**.

He makes lots of thick mucus in his lungs and digestive system. He has difficulty in breathing and absorbing food. There is no cure for cystic fibrosis. He needs daily physiotherapy to help clear the mucus from the lungs.

Cystic fibrosis is caused by a **recessive** gene. The cystic fibrosis gene was identified in 1989 and scientists have been able to identify the healthy allele of the gene. In 1990 scientists were able to replace the unhealthy allele with the healthy version in cells in a laboratory. The problem is finding a way of getting the healthy gene into a patient's cells.

b The boy's parents do not have cystic fibrosis, so how did he get it?

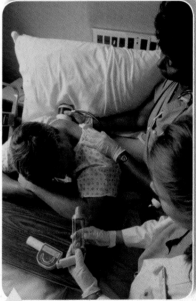

Cystic fibrosis

Summary Questions

1 Using gene therapy to treat cystic fibrosis is an example of genetic engineering. Use the internet to find out about other examples of genetic engineering.

2 Imagine you are a journalist in 1996. Write a news report about Dolly the sheep.

? KEY WORDS

clone

know your stuff

▼ Question 1 (level 3)

The drawing shows eight living things.

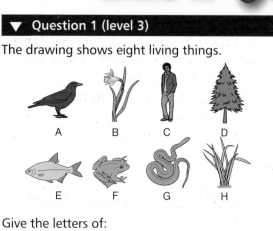

A   B   C   D

E   F   G   H

Give the letters of:

a *one* living thing which takes in oxygen through gills

b *one* living thing which makes seeds

c *one* living thing which breathes through lungs

d *two* living things which lay eggs in water

e *two* living things that are covered in scales. [7]

▼ Question 2 (level 4)

a The drawing below shows a sledge being pulled across ice by a team of huskies:

Huskies live in a cold climate. They pull a heavy sledge for a long time each day.

Choose *two* features from the list below that a dog breeder would look for when choosing huskies to breed from. Give the reason for each choice.

    blue eyes

    fierce nature

    long tail

    thick fur

    short legs

    strong muscles   [2]

b The drawings below show three dogs. They all look different.

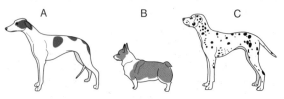

A   B   C

(i)   Which word describes the differences between these dogs?
Choose the correct word from the list:
adaptation   reproduction
variation   vaccination   [1]

(ii)   The drawing below shows a puppy. Dog C is the puppy's mother.

Why does the puppy look like his mother?   [1]

▼ Question 3 (level 7)

The quagga used to live in Africa. Quaggas belonged to the same group as zebras. They became extinct in about 1875. The drawings below show a zebra and a quagga.

zebra   quagga

Quaggas and zebras sometimes used to breed with each other. There are some zebras today that still have some quagga features. Scientists are using zebras to try to produce quaggas by selective breeding.

Describe the steps in this selective breeding process.   [3]

How Science Works

▼ Question 1 (level 4)

The chart shows a way to group living things.

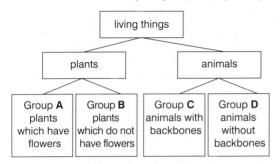

To which group, A, B, C or D, do the following living things belong?

Each letter may be used once, more than once or not at all.

slug   dog   daffodil   fern   [4]

▼ Question 2 (level 6)

Jamie and Freddie investigated variation in pupils in their year at school. First they measured the length of each pupil's little finger.

a Why did they make sure their little finger was straight while it was being measured?   [1]

b The bar chart shows their results.

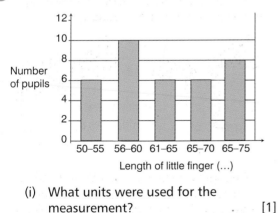

(i) What units were used for the measurement?   [1]

(ii) What is wrong with the way they grouped the finger lengths in their bar chart?   [1]

c Jamie and Freddie then counted the number of pupils who can roll their tongues. What method did they use to collect their data?

Observe pupils' tongues
Identify factors to keep the same
Look at books
Measure pupils' tongues.   [1]

d They recorded their results in a table.

Can roll tongue	Cannot roll tongue
10	4

Copy and complete the chart below to show how many pupils can roll their tongues.

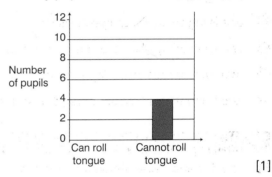

[1]

e Look at their bar charts for investigations 1 and 2. How can you tell that they used different numbers of pupils in each investigation?   [1]

f Two examples of variation were investigated. Which was an example of continuous variation and which was discontinuous variation?   [2]

Marvellous Metals

Marvellous metals

Metals are a very important group of substances, with many uses. You are probably wearing some metals, maybe in a zip or a piece of jewellery. Perhaps you have some coins with you?

a Write a list of things that you are wearing that contain a metal.

b What do iron, cobalt and nickel have in common?

Investigating properties of metals

In Fusion Book 1 you learned the differences between metals and non-metals. Most metals have similar properties. This can help scientists to classify quickly a material as a metal. You are going to refresh your memory about the properties of metals.

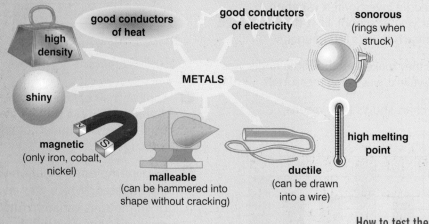

How to test the properties of metals

- Take a magnifying glass and look closely at the surface of the material. What is the surface of a metal like?
- Put your sample into water. Describe the density of most metals.
- Connect the material in a simple series circuit with a lamp and power supply. Turn on the power. Are metals conductors or insulators?
- Tap the material on the side of the bench. How would you describe the sound of a metal?
- Try to bend the metal. Using a nail, try to scratch the surface of the metal. What property of a metal does this demonstrate?
- Make a list of the general properties of a metal.

⚠ **Safety:** Crocodile clips can get hot. Do not damage the bench or your fingers.

H <small>Hydrogen</small>																	He <small>Helium</small>
Li <small>Lithium</small>	Be <small>Beryllium</small>											B <small>Boron</small>	C <small>Carbon</small>	N <small>Nitrogen</small>	O <small>Oxygen</small>	F <small>Fluorine</small>	Ne <small>Neon</small>
Na <small>Sodium</small>	Mg <small>Magnesium</small>											Al <small>Aluminium</small>	Si <small>Silicon</small>	P <small>Phosphorus</small>	S <small>Sulfur</small>	Cl <small>Chlorine</small>	Ar <small>Argon</small>
K <small>Potassium</small>	Ca <small>Calcium</small>	Sc <small>Scandium</small>	Ti <small>Titanium</small>	V <small>Vanadium</small>	Cr <small>Chromium</small>	Mn <small>Manganese</small>	Fe <small>Iron</small>	Co <small>Cobalt</small>	Ni <small>Nickel</small>	Cu <small>Copper</small>	Zn <small>Zinc</small>	Ga <small>Gallium</small>	Ge <small>Germanium</small>	As <small>Arsenic</small>	Se <small>Selenium</small>	Br <small>Bromine</small>	Kr <small>Krypton</small>
Rb <small>Rubidium</small>	Sr <small>Strontium</small>	Y <small>Yttrium</small>	Zr <small>Zirconium</small>	Nb <small>Niobium</small>	Mo <small>Molybdenum</small>	Tc <small>Technetium</small>	Ru <small>Ruthenium</small>	Rh <small>Rhodium</small>	Pd <small>Palladium</small>	Ag <small>Silver</small>	Cd <small>Cadmium</small>	In <small>Indium</small>	Sn <small>Tin</small>	Sb <small>Antimony</small>	Te <small>Tellurium</small>	I <small>Iodine</small>	Xe <small>Xenon</small>
Cs <small>Caesium</small>	Ba <small>Barium</small>	La <small>Lanthanum</small>	Hf <small>Hafnium</small>	Ta <small>Tantalum</small>	W <small>Tungsten</small>	Re <small>Rhenium</small>	Os <small>Osmium</small>	Ir <small>Iridium</small>	Pt <small>Platinum</small>	Au <small>Gold</small>	Hg <small>Mercury</small>	Tl <small>Thallium</small>	Pb <small>Lead</small>	Bi <small>Bismuth</small>	Po <small>Polonium</small>	At <small>Astatine</small>	Rn <small>Radon</small>
Fr <small>Francium</small>	Ra <small>Radium</small>	Ac <small>Actinium</small>															

	Ce <small>Cerium</small>	Pr <small>Praseodymium</small>	Nd <small>Neodymium</small>	Pm <small>Promethium</small>	Sm <small>Samarium</small>	Eu <small>Europium</small>	Gd <small>Gadolinium</small>	Tb <small>Terbium</small>	Dy <small>Dysprosium</small>	Ho <small>Holmium</small>	Er <small>Erbium</small>	Tm <small>Thulium</small>	Yb <small>Ytterbium</small>	Lu <small>Lutetium</small>
	Th <small>Thorium</small>	Pa <small>Protactinium</small>	U <small>Uranium</small>	Np <small>Neptunium</small>	Pu <small>Plutonium</small>	Am <small>Americium</small>	Cm <small>Curium</small>	Bk <small>Berkelium</small>	Cf <small>Californium</small>	Es <small>Einsteinium</small>	Fm <small>Fermium</small>	Md <small>Mendelevium</small>	No <small>Nobelium</small>	Lr <small>Lawrencium</small>

The Periodic Table of elements

Most elements are metals and are solids at room temperature. All metals are found on the left-hand side and centre of the Periodic Table.

Non-metals are another group of substances. Most non-metals have the opposite properties to most metals. These elements are found on the right-hand side of the Periodic Table.

G List the properties of non-metals.

The metalloid silicon is used to make computer chips in this factory

Great Debates

'Metals are more important than non-metals.' Have a vote on this, then discuss it and vote again.

Stretch Yourself

Some elements are called metalloids (meaning 'metal-like'). These are found on the border between metals and non-metals in the Periodic Table, often shown as a dark line like a staircase (see page 74). They have some of the properties of metals, and some of the properties of non-metals. Metalloids include silicon used in computer chips and mobile phones. Can you find some other examples of metalloids?

Metals and Oxygen

▶▶ What happens when a metal reacts with oxygen?

▶▶ Do all metals react with oxygen?

Oxidation

About one-fifth of the air is oxygen. Some metals can react with oxygen if they are left in the air. This chemical reaction is known as **oxidation** and a **metal oxide** is made. The general word equation for this reaction is:

$$\text{metal} + \text{oxygen} \longrightarrow \text{metal oxide}$$

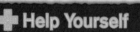
Magnesium has different properties from magnesium oxide

ⓐ What are the reactants in the general equation above?

ⓑ What is the product in the general equation above?

A metal oxide will have different properties from the metal that it is made from. This could affect the performance of the metal and so also affect the job it can be used for.

ⓒ What percentage of the air is oxygen?

ⓓ Copy and complete the following word equation:
calcium + oxygen ⟶ ...

➕ Help Yourself

Think back to Fusion Book 1. Can you remember how to test for oxygen?

Some reactive metals like sodium cannot be stored in air as they oxidise quickly. These reactive metals are stored under oil. This means that the metal is kept in a bottle of oil. The oil protects the metal from oxygen and water in the air. Even more reactive metals, such as caesium are kept in sealed vials with a noble gas. Can you explain why?

Not all metals react with oxygen in the air, even at very high temperatures. Gold is a very unreactive metal and does not react with oxygen. This is one of the reasons it is used in jewellery. The gold remains chemically unchanged in air.

Reactive metals are kept under oil

activity

Investigating the reaction of metals and oxygen

Following a terrorist attack on 11 September 2001, the Twin Towers of the World Trade Centre in New York collapsed. Thousands of people lost their lives. It was discovered that the skyscraper eventually collapsed because the steel structure was damaged by heat. But, even at these high temperatures all of the steel did not oxidise.

It is important for designers to know how metals are affected by oxygen, so that they can choose the correct metal for a job. You are going to investigate the **rate** of oxidation. Rate is the speed of a chemical reaction.

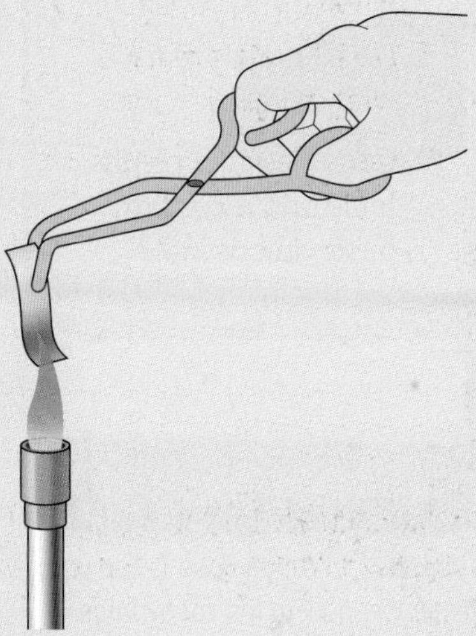

- Make a prediction about the rate of oxidation of a metal in air and the same metal in a gas jar full of oxygen.
- Set up a Bunsen burner and safety equipment.
- Measure a 2 cm length of magnesium ribbon.
- Using tongs, hold the magnesium ribbon in the blue Bunsen flame until it catches light, and then remove from the heat, keeping it above the heat proof mat.

Safety: Do not look directly at the burning magnesium. Wear eye protection.

- Observe the reaction through blue cobalt glass.
- With a new 2 cm length of magnesium ribbon, wind it into a corkscrew shape and put it onto a deflagrating spoon, with an edge sticking out.
- Heat the magnesium until it catches light and put it into a gas jar of oxygen.
- Observe the reaction through blue cobalt glass.
- Repeat the two reactions using iron wool.
- Record your observations in a table.
- What conclusion can you draw from this experiment?

Summary Questions

1. Copy and complete the passage using the words below:

   metal increased oxygen chemical oxidation

   Some metals will react with oxygen in the air to form a ... oxide. This change produces a new substance, and so it is an irreversible, ... change. The reaction between a metal and ... is an example of an oxidation reaction. The rate, or speed of the ... can be increased if the percentage of oxygen in the air is... .

2. Copy and complete the following word equations:

   a) sodium + oxygen ⟶ ...

   b) iron + ... ⟶ iron oxide

   c) ... + oxygen ⟶ aluminium oxide

3. Aluminium is quite a reactive metal, but we can use it to wrap up food without it reacting with the food or the air. Find out how aluminium is protected from reacting with oxygen in the air.

Did You Know?

It is possible to make gold oxide using plasma made from oxygen. Plasma is often called the fourth state of matter and is a form of very high energy gas.

KEY WORDS

oxidation
metal oxide
rate

Metals and Water

Reactions with water

When some metals come into contact with water a new substance is made. The chemical reaction between a metal and water will produce a **metal hydroxide** and hydrogen gas. The general equation for this reaction is:

metal + water ⟶ metal hydroxide + hydrogen

> **a** Copy and complete the following word equation:
>
> sodium + water ⟶ ...

Metal hydroxides belong to a group of chemicals called **bases**. This means they react with acids. If the metal hydroxide can dissolve in water, like sodium hydroxide, it is also called an **alkali**. The alkaline solution formed will have a pH greater than 7.

✚ Help Yourself

Think back to Fusion Book 1. Can you remember how to test for hydrogen?

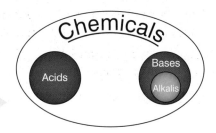

A Venn diagram to show how chemicals can be classified

Chemicals

Acids

Bases

Alkalis

Did You Know?

When magnesium reacts with cold water, hydrogen and magnesium hydroxide are produced very slowly. But, when magnesium reacts with steam, magnesium oxide and hydrogen are made in a vigorous reaction.

> **b** List a similarity and a difference between bases and alkalis.

activity

Demonstration

Group 1 metals are also known as 'alkali metals'. These are very reactive metals and have few uses as the metals themselves, but lots of uses when they are in compounds. Your teacher is going to demonstrate the reaction between water and the first three Group 1 metals. You need to design a results table to record your observations.

I'm glad I didn't discover Caesium!

Caesium, from Group 1, is too reactive to use in schools

Potassium reacting with water (which has universal indicators added)

> **c** How do you make observations?

Reactions of metals with water

When a designer is planning a building, it is important that they know the properties of the materials they plan to use. Any materials that are outside, may get wet. This makes it important that they do not react quickly, or at all, with water. You are going to investigate the metals calcium, magnesium and copper and list them in order of reactivity.

- Almost fill a small beaker with water.
- Put a water-filled test tube upside down in the water.
- Using a spatula drop a piece of calcium into the water.
- Collect the gas given off in the test tube.
- Record your observations in a table.
- Remove the tube of gas and test it with a lighted splint. If you hear a pop, you have collected hydrogen.
- With a new sample of water, repeat for each metal.
- **Safety:** Do not touch calcium, or the solution it forms, with your hands, wear eye protection.
- How can you tell which is the most reactive metal?
- Order the metals from this experiment, and the demonstration that the teacher did, from most reactive to least reactive.
- **Extension:** You might want to add universal indicator to the water. What do you predict will happen?

Summary Questions

1 Match the correct endings to the following sentences:

a) Hydrogen and a metal hydroxide are	is a soluble base.
b) A base and an alkali	when sodium reacts with water.
c) An alkali	made when a metal reacts with water.
d) Sodium hydroxide and hydrogen are made	will react with an acid.

2 Copy and complete the following word equations:

a) lithium + water $\longrightarrow$ ... + hydrogen

b) caesium + ... $\longrightarrow$ caesium hydroxide + hydrogen

c) ... + water $\longrightarrow$ calcium hydroxide + hydrogen

KEY WORDS

metal hydroxide
base
alkali

Metals and Acid

▸▸ What happens when a metal reacts with acid?

▸▸ Do all metals react with acid?

➕ Help Yourself

Think back to Fusion Book 1. Can you remember the names of some strong acids and some weak acids?

Reaction between zinc and acid

Stretch Yourself

The acid particle is actually H^+(aq). This is a hydrogen ion that has been dissolved into water. An ion is an atom that has a positive or negative charge.

Reactions with acid

A chemical reaction can happen when some metals come into contact with an **acid**. The products of the reaction are a **metal salt** and hydrogen gas. The general equation for this reaction is:

metal + acid $\longrightarrow$ **metal salt + hydrogen**

Rain is carbonic acid. Not all metals will react with all acids!

ⓐ Look carefully at the photograph of zinc reacting with acid. What observations tell you a gas has been made?

If you think of any acid that you have used, e.g. hydrochloric acid (HCl), nitric acid (HNO_3) and carbonic acid (H_2CO_3), they all contain hydrogen. A metal salt is made when hydrogen in an acid is swapped for a metal. For example, if hydrochloric acid reacts with sodium then sodium chloride (NaCl), a metal salt is made. The hydrogen has been swapped for the metal. Why do you think this reaction is never done in a school lab?

This table will help you name the metal salts produced from the reaction between a metal and common acids:

Acid	Name of salt
Hydrochloric acid	Metal chloride
Nitric acid	Metal nitrate
Phosphoric acid	Metal phosphate
Sulfuric acid	Metal sulfate

ⓑ Complete the following word equation:

magnesium + nitric acid $\longrightarrow$ ...

Reacting metals with acids

Many acids are found in foods. It is important that food cans do not react with our food, as this would be expensive and some of the compounds that would be made could be dangerous to eat. You are going to investigate the metals magnesium, tin and zinc.

- Using a measuring cylinder, put $3\,cm^3$ of dilute hydrochloric acid into a test tube.

- Using a piece of sandpaper, rub the surface of each metal.

- Why do you sandpaper the surface of the metal?

- Drop a piece of magnesium into the acid.

- Record your observations into a table.

- With a new sample of acid, repeat for each metal.

⚠ **Safety:** Wear eye protection.

- How can you tell which is the most reactive metal?

- Order the metals from this experiment from most reactive to least reactive.

- Which metal would you use to make food cans from? Explain your answer.

- **Extension:** What do you predict would happen if you used a different acid in this experiment? Why not try it out to see if your prediction is right?

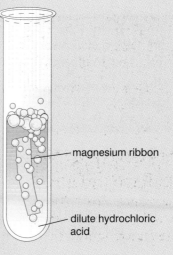

magnesium ribbon

dilute hydrochloric acid

Summary Questions

❶ Copy and complete the following sentences:
  a) Some metals like magnesium can …
  b) Hydrogen is made …
  c) A metal salt is …

❷ Copy and complete the following word equations:
  a) calcium + nitric acid $\longrightarrow$ … + hydrogen
  b) iron + hydrochloric acid $\longrightarrow$ iron chloride + …
  c) zinc + … $\longrightarrow$ zinc nitrate + hydrogen

❸ Write word equations for all the chemical reactions in the activity above.

❹ Find out what metals are used to make cutlery. Explain why these metals are used.

KEY WORDS

metal salt
acid

Reactivity Series

▶▶ Are some metals more reactive than others?

▶▶ What is the reactivity series?

Order of reactivity

The most reactive elements, such as calcium (Ca), will chemically change in oxygen, water or acid. The least reactive **metals**, like copper (Cu), will not react with oxygen, water or acid. Some metals, such as zinc (Zn), will react with acid but not with cold water. We can use these observations to make a league table of the metals. This list is called the **reactivity series**.

Reactions of Ca, Cu and Zn with acid ▶

The reactivity series

K	potassium
Na	sodium
Li	lithium
Ca	calcium
Mg	magnesium
Al	aluminium
Zn	zinc
Fe	iron
Sn	tin
Pb	lead
Cu	copper
Ag	silver
Au	gold
Pt	platinum

The reactivity series is a list of elements starting with the most reactive and going down to the least reactive. The reactivity series is a list made up mainly of metals. We can find out the order of the elements by observing any chemical reactions that happen between the element and acid, water or oxygen and making a note of the **reactivity** of that element. The elements are then listed in order from the most to the least reactive.

ⓐ Which metal is more reactive than calcium, but less reactive than sodium?

The reactivity series can be used to make predictions. You would not use a metal high up in the reactivity series for jewellery, as it would probably react with water and oxygen in the air, not to mention acids in rain water. The jewellery would not last long!

ⓑ Give an example of a metal that you might use for jewellery.

Reactive metals have very few uses!

activity

The reactivity series

- Look back at pages 51–61 and the results from the experiments and demonstrations of metals reacting with oxygen, water and acid. Order the metals that you have studied from the most to least reactive to make your own version of the reactivity series.

- Which is the most reactive metal that you have studied?

- Which is the least reactive metal that you have studied?

Did You Know?

Some versions of the reactivity series also list carbon and hydrogen. Any elements listed above hydrogen will react with an acid.

Summary Questions

1 Match the key word to its correct definition:

a) Reactivity series	A chemical that is shiny, malleable and a conductor. They often have high melting and boiling points and are sonorous.
b) Reactivity	A list of elements from the most reactive to the least reactive.
c) Metal	An indication of how likely a chemical is to undergo a chemical change.

2 Where would you put caesium in the reactivity series? Explain your answer.

3 Copper, silver and gold will not react with an acid, but lead and tin react slowly with warm acid to give hydrogen gas and a metal salt. Where would you put hydrogen in the reactivity series? Explain your answer.

THE BELVEDERE ACADEMY
SCIENCE DEPARTMENT

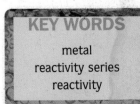

KEY WORDS

metal
reactivity series
reactivity

Solid Displacement

- ▸▸ What is displacement?
- ▸▸ Can one solid metal displace another metal from its solid metal compounds?

Did You Know?

Displacement means moving from one place to another. In science, displacement means one element has 'pushed out' another element from a compound.

When iron and copper compete, iron is more reactive and will 'win' the place in the compound

Displacement reactions

A more reactive element will displace a less reactive element from its compounds. This is an example of a chemical reaction because new substances are made. This type of chemical change is called a **displacement** reaction.

> ⓐ Give an example of a metal that would displace copper from its compound.

Thermite reaction

Railway lines are made in lengths and they have to be joined on the track side. It would be very difficult to get molten iron to the track. So railway workers make the molten metal where they need it. They mix aluminium and iron oxide in a special container and add a flare to get the displacement reaction started. The aluminium displaces the iron from iron oxide and molten iron and aluminium oxide are made.

Your teacher is going to demonstrate the thermite reaction.

- Write a word equation for the displacement reaction.
- What do you observe?

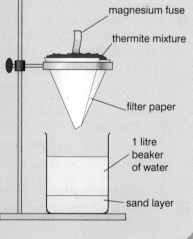

magnesium fuse

thermite mixture

filter paper

1 litre beaker of water

sand layer

In a solid displacement reaction it is important to mix the chemicals well. This is so the particles of the reactants are close together to allow the chemical reaction to happen. The reaction will also need heat energy to get it started. This starting energy is called **activation energy**.

Predicting reactions

You can use the reactivity series to predict the products of a displacement reaction. Look up the metals in the reactants in the series. The metal that is higher in the reactivity series will end up in the compound. If that metal is already in the reactant compound then no displacement reaction will happen. If the most reactive metal is on its own as a reactant, then it will 'steal' the place in the compound, releasing the other metal.

The reactivity series

Think about magnesium and copper oxide being well mixed and heated. Magnesium is higher in the reactivity series than copper, and so it can bond more strongly to the oxygen atom. This means that copper is displaced from the copper oxide, making copper and magnesium oxide. The word equation would be:

magnesium + copper oxide $\longrightarrow$ magnesium oxide + copper

ⓑ Complete the following word equation:

magnesium + iron oxide $\longrightarrow$ ...

Stretch Yourself

Displacement reactions are exothermic reactions. This means that they release energy during the reaction, mostly as heat. List some other exothermic reactions that you have studied.

Summary Questions

❶ Copy and complete the passage using the words below:

elements   compound   displacement   new   chemical

More reactive elements will 'push out' less reactive ... from their compound. This is called a ... reaction, as the more reactive element has displaced, or moved, the less reactive element from the ... Displacement reactions are an example of a ... change because ... substances are made.

❷ Copy and complete the following word equations:
a)   magnesium + zinc oxide $\longrightarrow$ ... + zinc
b)   iron + copper oxide $\longrightarrow$ iron oxide + ...
c)   ... + aluminium oxide $\longrightarrow$ magnesium oxide aluminium
d)   sodium oxide + magnesium $\longrightarrow$ ...

❸ Find out what copper thermite is and what it can be used for.

KEY WORDS

displacement
thermite
activation energy

Solution Displacement

▸▸ Can one solid metal displace another metal from a solution?

▸▸ How can I predict the outcome of a reaction using the reactivity series?

Displacement in solution

Many metal compounds will dissolve in water to make a **solution**. If a more reactive metal is put into a solution of a less reactive metal compound, then a **displacement** reaction will happen.

In solution displacement, you do not need to mix the reactants. This is because the particles of the metal compound are mixed thoroughly with water particles. So the metal compound particles are always moving and eventually they will collide with the metal particles.

ⓐ Why do you not need to mix the reactants in solution displacement reactions?

In a solution displacement reaction, you may observe colour changes. The metal solution may change colour as a different metal compound is made, or the solid metal changes colour as a different metal has been made. A chemical reaction that happens without any extra energy being added is called a **spontaneous** reaction.

When copper and silver nitrate meet, copper nitrate and silver are made

ⓑ Look carefully at the photograph of the reaction between copper and silver nitrate. What observations tell you that a chemical reaction has happened?

activity

Solution displacement

Displacement reactions can be used in electrochemical cells. Electrochemical cells are stores of chemical energy and when the chemical reaction starts, the energy can be converted into electrical energy. In these cells, it is important to choose the correct chemicals so that enough energy is stored. You are going to investigate four metals and their solutions to discover the order of reactivity.

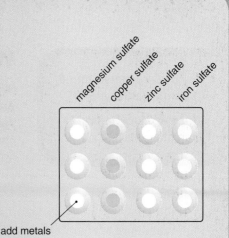

magnesium sulfate   copper sulfate   zinc sulfate   iron sulfate

⚠ Safety: Wear eye protection.

- In a dimple dish add magnesium sulfate solution to three dimples. In the first dimple add a piece of copper, in the second a piece of zinc and in the third a piece of iron.

  add metals

- Add copper sulfate solution to three clean dimples. Put a piece of magnesium, zinc and iron in separate dimples with the copper sulfate solution in.

- Add zinc sulfate solution to three clean dimples. Put a piece of magnesium, copper and iron in separate dimples with the zinc sulfate solution in.

- Add iron sulfate solution to three clean dimples. Put a piece of magnesium, copper and zinc in separate dimples with the iron sulfate solution in.

- Now record which dimples have had a chemical reaction.

- Why was a metal sulfate used in all the chemical reactions?

- List the metals from the most reactive to the least reactive.

Summary Questions

1 Match the key word to its correct definition:

a) Solution displacement	A type of mixture.
b) Spontaneous	A chemical reaction that happens without any extra activation energy being added.
c) Solution	A more reactive metal will displace a less reactive metal from its compound which has been dissolved in water.

2 Copy and complete the following word equations:

a)   magnesium + zinc nitrate ⟶ ... + zinc

b)   iron + silver nitrate ⟶ iron nitrate + ...

c)   ... + silver nitrate ⟶ silver + magnesium nitrate

3 Write a flow chart to explain how you can predict the products of a solution displacement reaction.

KEY WORDS

solution
solution displacement
spontaneous

Extraction of Metals

C1.8

> ▶▶ How are metals found in the Earth's crust?
>
> ▶▶ How can we extract metals?

Where do we get metals from?

We can dig unreactive metals from the Earth's crust. These metals are called native metals and include gold and silver. They do not react with elements in the environment and this is why we can find the pure metal.

Gold is a native metal and can be found in nuggets

a Write the symbol of a native metal.

We find reactive metals in compounds in the Earth's crust. These compounds are called **minerals**. Most minerals are oxides or sulfides of the metal. If there is enough of the metal to be economic to extract it, the mineral is also called an **ore**. Metals can only be **extracted** from a mineral using a chemical reaction; this type of chemical change is called reduction.

Haematite is mainly iron oxide and is an example of a mineral and an ore

b What are the similarities and differences between an ore and a mineral?

Any metal below carbon in the reactivity series can be extracted by displacement with carbon. An impure form of carbon like coal, coke or charcoal is mixed with the mineral and then it is heated. This process is called **smelting**.

Smelting

activity

Smelting is a traditional way of extracting metals from minerals. Smelting was probably first done by accident, when a camp fire was made on top of lead or tin ores. The first smelted metal is believed to be lead and was found in Turkey. It dated from 6500 BC. You are going to smelt some lead.

- Mix one spatula of carbon powder with a spatula of lead oxide.
- Put the mixture in a boiling tube and add a plug of mineral wool.
- Heat the mixture in the hottest part of the Bunsen flame.

  ⚠ **Safety:** Wear eye protection and take care with hot glass.

- After a few minutes tip the mixture into an evaporating dish.
- What do you observe?
- Write a word equation for this reaction.

  ⚠ **Safety:** Wear eye protection and remember that lead oxide is toxic.

loose plug of mineral wool (to stop mixture shooting out)

mixture of carbon and lead oxide

heat

Stretch Yourself

Highly reactive metals can only be extracted using electricity in a process called electrolysis. Two electrodes are put into the molten metal compound and electricity is passed through it. The metal is collected at the negative electrode (cathode) and non-metal in the compound is collected at the positive electrode (anode). Why do you think this method of extraction is so expensive?

Aluminium extraction

Summary Questions

1 Match the correct endings to the following sentences:

a)	Extracting metal from its ore	are all examples of native metals.
b)	Iron can be extracted	is an example of a reduction reaction.
c)	Gold, silver and platinum	from haematite by smelting.
d)	Highly reactive metals can only be	extracted from their ores using electrolysis.

2 Copy and complete the following word equations for smelting reactions:

a) copper oxide + carbon $\longrightarrow$ ... + carbon dioxide

b) iron oxide + carbon $\longrightarrow$ iron + ...

c) zinc oxide + ... $\longrightarrow$ zinc + carbon dioxide

3 Make a poster to explain how iron is extracted from haematite in the blast furnace. Try to include chemical reactions that happen in the industrial process.

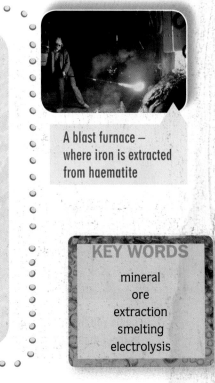

A blast furnace – where iron is extracted from haematite

KEY WORDS

mineral
ore
extraction
smelting
electrolysis

What's the Damage? (1)

- ▸▸ Should we keep extracting metals from the Earth's crust?
- ▸▸ Should we keep refining metals?

Panning for gold

Could you live life without metals?

Environmental impact

Some metals and minerals can be collected from the surface of the Earth. Native metals can be eroded from rocks and the particles find their way into streams and river. **Panning** for gold is one of the most traditional methods of gathering the metal. Panning involves swirling river water in a pan. Gold has a higher density than most sediment and water. This means that the gold collects in the centre at the bottom of the pan.

a What is erosion?

Most metals and metal ores must be mined or quarried. A quarry is a large open air excavation often dug out from the side of a rockface or mountain and sometimes is called an open cast mine. A mine is a series of tunnels dug into rocks. Both mining and quarrying involve removing many tonnes of waste rock for a few tonnes of useful metal or metal ore.

Swedish iron ore mine

Open cast iron oxide mine in Brazil

Metal extraction creates new jobs for the local community and attracts more money to build better roads and rail networks. However, mining and quarrying can be dangerous work, with many workers losing their lives when mines collapse. They can cause air, noise and visual **pollution**. Also tunnels in the ground can cause buildings to become unsteady and begin to crack as they fall into the Earth. This is called subsidence.

b What are the differences and similarities between mining and quarrying?

GEOGRAPHY

Mining involves removing a raw material to be used in manufacturing. This means that mining is an example of a primary industry. The UK shut down much of its primary industry during the 20th century, with most people now being employed in the tertiary sector, which includes all jobs in tourism and IT.

Lots of miners lost their jobs in the 1980's when most UK mines closed

When metals are extracted and purified, we often need other chemicals, such as coke. This means that we need to transport all the raw materials to a factory, often by road. At the factory, the metal is extracted leaving many more tonnes of waste. Sometimes the waste can be sold on and used; at other times it is just released into the environment. As we extract more and more metals, it gets harder to find ores with a high percentage of metal in them and so we need to dispose of even more waste material.

Great Debates

Imagine that a big deposit of a metal ore had been discovered just 10 miles from your house. The ore was 50 metres below ground on farm land. The farmer could no longer make enough money from farming his dairy cows and has re-trained and works as a teacher in a local school. Do you think that the land should be quarried, mined or left alone? Explain your opinion.

Did You Know?

Slag is a waste material from the extraction of iron from haematite (iron oxide). Slag is used to make breeze blocks, road bases and building materials.

Stretch Yourself

Electrolysis is used to extract reactive metals from their metal ores. The electricity is a secondary source of energy. This means it is generated somewhere else, often from fossil fuels and causes pollution at the power station. Do you think we should keep extracting reactive metals?

Summary Questions

1 Match the key word to its correct definition:

a)	Panning	A large open air excavation often dug out from the side of a rockface or mountain.
b)	Mine	A method for extracting small particles of eroded native metals from a stream or river.
c)	Quarry	A series of tunnels used to extract natural resources from the Earth.
d)	Pollution	Changes to an ecosystem caused by humans. This could include changes to light, heat, noise, chemicals, etc.

2 On an outline of the map of the UK, show where silver, tin, lead, copper and gold can be found.

KEY WORDS

panning
mine
quarry
pollution

Metal Corrosion

- What is metal corrosion?
- What is rusting?
- What causes rusting?
- How should I evaluate an experiment?

Corrosion is a chemical change between a metal and substances in the environment. This chemical reaction makes a new substance and so it changes the overall properties of the material.

a How can you tell that a copper roof has corroded?

Rusting

Corrosion of iron is called **rusting** and is a slow chemical change using oxygen and water. Only materials that contain iron, such as steel, can rust. Look at the chart below to see how we try to stop rusting:

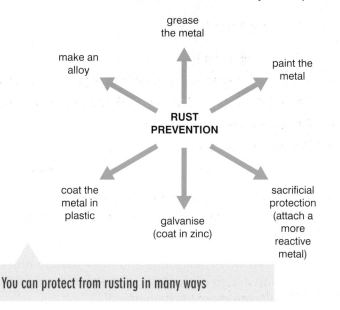

grease the metal

make an alloy

paint the metal

RUST PREVENTION

coat the metal in plastic

galvanise (coat in zinc)

sacrificial protection (attach a more reactive metal)

You can protect from rusting in many ways

Copper can be used for roofs, but it quickly corrodes to a form of copper carbonate

Did You Know?

Rust is a brown compound made of hydrated iron oxide.

b What two substances are needed for rusting to happen?

Evaluation

When an experiment is evaluated you review what you have done and the results that you have collected. You should highlight any **anomalous** results and comment on the reliability and accuracy of your data. **Reliable** results are very similar every time you repeat the experiment. You can trust reliable results, so repeating readings can make results more reliable. However, if you make the same mistake each time you repeat a test, your results will still not be accurate. **Accurate** results are close to the true values. Anomalous results do not fit the pattern of data.

Link up to...

DESIGN AND TECHNOLOGY

Oxidation reactions can cause food to go off. Some packaged foods are sold with little sachets of iron in their packaging. The iron reacts with any oxygen, forming rust. This means there is no oxygen left to react with the food and this increases shelf life.

c What is the difference between accurate results and reliable results?

activity

Rusting experiment

A car body that is very rusted will fail its MOT (certificate to prove that it is safe to drive on UK roads). This is because in a crash, the car would not have the same strength as it would if there were no rust there. You are going to investigate the conditions needed for rusting.

- Get four test tubes marked A to D and put them in a test tube rack.
- Add an identical iron nail to each test tube.

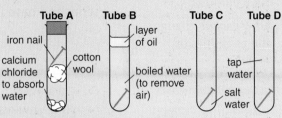

- In each test tube add:

  A: A spatula of calcium chloride (drying agent) and a bung.

  B: 10 cm³ of boiled water (all dissolved gases are removed) and a layer of oil.

  C: 10 cm³ of salt water.

  D: 10 cm³ of tap water.

- Predict the results using science to explain your ideas.
- Leave the test tubes for one week and record the results in a table.
- Was your prediction correct?
- Evaluate your experiment.

Think about your experiment: explain the causes of any anomalous results and suggest how you would prevent them from happening again.

Summary Questions

1 Copy and complete the passage using the words below:

steel **rusting** **metal** **chemical** **water**

Corrosion is a chemical reaction between a … and substances in its environment. Rusting is an example of a … reaction that can only happen to iron. As steel contains iron, … can also rust. For … to happen, both oxygen and … must be present.

2 Salt increases the speed or rate of rusting.

  a) Most car bodies are made of steel. Explain why it is important that car owners near the seaside wash their cars more frequently than if they lived inland.

  b) Explain why it is important for car owners near the seaside to paint over any scratches on their car as soon as they notice them.

3 Find out the formula(s) for rust.

What's the Use?

» How do we decide which metal is suitable for a particular use?

» How can we change the properties of metals?

Using metals

The most reactive metals are found in Groups 1 and 2 of the Periodic Table. These elements are listed high up in the reactivity series and have few uses as pure metals. However, their compounds are useful.

- metals
- non-metals
- semi-metals or metalloids

H 1 hydrogen																	He 2 helium
Li 3 lithium	Be 4 beryllium											B 5 boron	C 6 carbon	N 7 nitrogen	O 8 oxygen	F 9 fluorine	Ne 10 neon
Na 11 sodium	Mg 12 magnesium											Al 13 aluminium	Si 14 silicon	P 15 phosphorus	S 16 sulfur	Cl 17 chlorine	Ar 18 argon
K 19 potassium	Ca 20 calcium	Sc 21 scandium	Ti 22 titanium	V 23 vanadium	Cr 24 chromium	Mn 25 manganese	Fe 26 iron	Co 27 cobalt	Ni 28 nickel	Cu 29 copper	Zn 30 zinc	Ga 31 gallium	Ge 32 germanium	As 33 arsenic	Se 34 selenium	Br 35 bromine	Kr 36 krypton
Rb 37 rubidium	Sr 38 strontium	Y 39 yttrium	Zr 40 zirconium	Nb 41 niobium	Mo 42 molybdenum	Tc 43 technetium	Ru 44 ruthenium	Rh 45 rhodium	Pd 46 palladium	Ag 47 silver	Cd 48 cadmium	In 49 indium	Sn 50 tin	Sb 51 antimony	Te 52 tellurium	I 53 iodine	Xe 54 xenon
Cs 55 caesium	Ba 56 barium	La 57 lanthanum	Hf 72 hafnium	Ta 73 tantalum	W 74 tungsten	Re 75 rhenium	Os 76 osmium	Ir 77 iridium	Pt 78 platinum	Au 79 gold	Hg 80 mercury	Tl 81 thallium	Pb 82 lead	Bi 83 bismuth	Po 84 polonium	At 85 astatine	Rn 86 radon

Metals are found on the left of the Periodic Table

a Where are the most reactive metals found in the Periodic Table?

Metals in the central part of the Periodic Table are called **transition metals**. These metals are often quite unreactive and can have many uses because of their properties. Titanium, (Ti), is a transition metal that is strong with a low density. Titanium can be used in medicine.

CAREERS

Barium sulfate is a white compound that some patients are given to drink before being X-rayed. Barium sulfate and bones stop X-rays but X-rays pass through other cells in the body. This lets medical technicians see the inside of your digestive system more clearly. If you drink the compound it is called a 'barium meal', if the compound is pushed up your bottom it is called an 'enema'.

For example, titanium can be used to make artificial hip joints

b What are transition metals?

c Think about the properties of titanium. What could be some uses of titanium?

activity

Alloys

Pure metals such as gold are elements. All the atoms are the same and they can have some properties that we might not find useful. Gold is a very soft metal as the layers of atoms can easily slide past each other. If a small amount of another element is added, then a solid mixture called an **alloy** is made. A gold alloy is harder than pure gold because the atoms cannot slide past each other as easily because there is the odd atom of a different size in the way. You are going to make a model of a pure metal and an alloy.

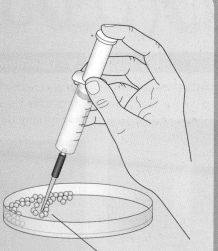

a bubble raft (a Petri dish containing a solution of washing-up-liquid)

- Half-fill a Petri dish with soap solution.
- Using a pipette, blow same sized bubbles to cover the surface.
- Push a layer of bubbles with the tip of the pipette, what do you notice?
- Now add a few new bigger bubbles to the dish.
- Push a layer of bubbles, what do you notice?
- Which model is a pure metal and which model is an alloy? Why is this model useful?

Did You Know?

Iron is a transition metal that is needed by your body to make red blood cells. Iron metal is added to breakfast cereal. When the iron reaches your stomach, some of it will react with the acid to make iron chloride. This can be absorbed by your body and used. The rest of the iron just passes through!

Stretch Yourself

Transition metals also have a special property that makes them useful as catalysts. Catalysts change the speed of a chemical reaction. Palladium and platinum can be found in catalytic converters. These converters change harmful waste gases from a car exhaust to gases already found in our atmosphere. We need to carry out lots of experiments to find a suitable catalyst for a particular reaction. But, once found, the catalyst can be used over and over again as it does not get used up itself in the reaction. Find out what chemical reactions happen in a catalytic converter.

A catalytic converter

Summary Questions

❶ Match the key word to its correct definition:

a) Transition metals	A solid mixture, made mainly of metals.
b) Alloy	A chemical that changes the rate of a chemical reaction but remains chemically unchanged itself at the end of the reaction.
c) Catalyst	Elements found in the middle block of the Periodic Table.

❷ Steel is an alloy of mainly iron with different elements added. Mild steel contains 0.2% carbon and is soft, medium steel contains between 0.3% and 0.6% carbon and is hard, and high-carbon steel contains 0.6 to 1.5% carbon and is very hard.

  a) Show this data in a table.

  b) What is the relationship between the amount of carbon and the hardness of steel?

KEY WORDS

transition metal
alloy
catalyst

know your stuff

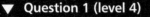

▼ Question 1 (level 4)

Murphy observed the reaction between sodium metal and water.

ⓐ What observation could Murphy use to conclude that a chemical change was happening? Use the picture to help you. [1]

ⓑ Which gas would be made in this reaction? Choose one of the following.

oxygen   hydrogen   carbon dioxide [1]

ⓒ Explain how you could use a splint to prove which gas is being made. [2]

▼ Question 2 (level 5)

Elements can be grouped as metals or non-metals. Iron is an example of a metal element.

ⓐ Which is **not** a property of iron? Choose one of the following.

good electrical conductor
shiny   magnetic
good thermal insulator [1]

ⓑ When iron is left out in the air, it reacts with oxygen to make hydrated iron oxide. What is the common name for this chemical? [1]

ⓒ When iron filings are sprinkled into a Bunsen burner flame, a chemical reaction happens. Copy and complete the word equation for this reaction:

… + … ⟶ iron oxide [2]

ⓓ What type of chemical reaction is this? [1]

▼ Question 3 (level 6):

Metals can be found in the Earth's crust. The metals are mined, purified and then used to make many different products.

ⓐ Use the words below to copy and complete the passage that follows. You may use the words more than once.

silver   aluminium   mineral(s)
compound   element

Unreactive metals like gold, … and platinum can be found as a pure … in the Earth's crust. These metals are known as native metals.

Most metals are found in … Minerals are made mainly of a metal … If there is enough metal in a mineral to make it economic to extract, the … is also called an ore. Bauxite is an example of an … ore. [6]

ⓑ Give an example of a chemical method for extracting a metal from its ore. [1]

▼ Question 4 (level 7):

Railway lines are welded together using the thermite reaction. Aluminium powder and iron oxide are the two reactants that are used to make pure iron.

ⓐ Write a word equation for this reaction. [2]

ⓑ What type of chemical change has happened? [1]

ⓒ Explain why this chemical change happens. [2]

How Science Works

▼ Question 1 (level 4)

Stella and Poppy wanted to find out what was needed for rusting to happen. They set up the following test tubes:

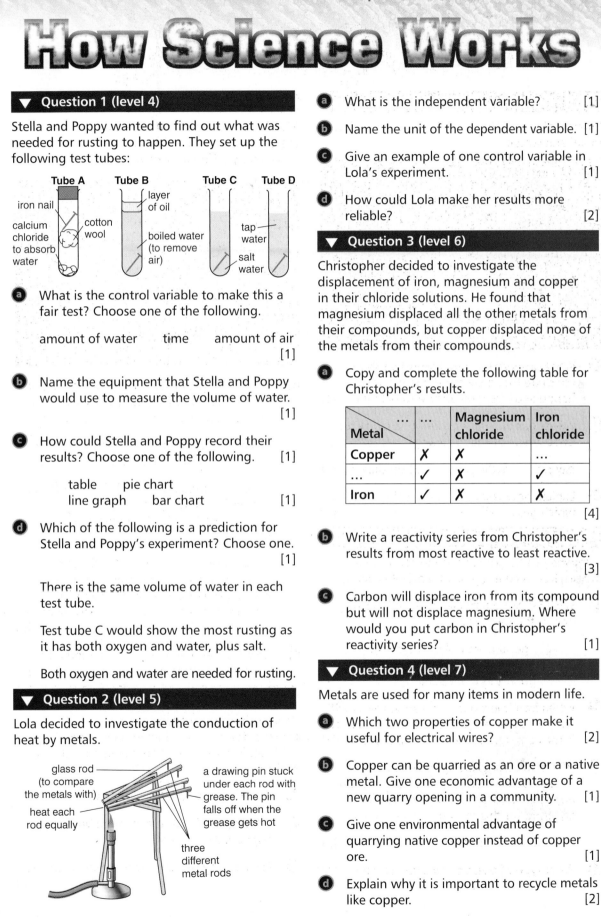

a What is the control variable to make this a fair test? Choose one of the following.

amount of water   time   amount of air [1]

b Name the equipment that Stella and Poppy would use to measure the volume of water. [1]

c How could Stella and Poppy record their results? Choose one of the following. [1]

table   pie chart
line graph   bar chart [1]

d Which of the following is a prediction for Stella and Poppy's experiment? Choose one. [1]

There is the same volume of water in each test tube.

Test tube C would show the most rusting as it has both oxygen and water, plus salt.

Both oxygen and water are needed for rusting.

▼ Question 2 (level 5)

Lola decided to investigate the conduction of heat by metals.

a What is the independent variable? [1]

b Name the unit of the dependent variable. [1]

c Give an example of one control variable in Lola's experiment. [1]

d How could Lola make her results more reliable? [2]

▼ Question 3 (level 6)

Christopher decided to investigate the displacement of iron, magnesium and copper in their chloride solutions. He found that magnesium displaced all the other metals from their compounds, but copper displaced none of the metals from their compounds.

a Copy and complete the following table for Christopher's results.

Metal	... ...	Magnesium chloride	Iron chloride
Copper	✗	✗	...
...	✓	✗	✓
Iron	✓	✗	✗

[4]

b Write a reactivity series from Christopher's results from most reactive to least reactive. [3]

c Carbon will displace iron from its compound but will not displace magnesium. Where would you put carbon in Christopher's reactivity series? [1]

▼ Question 4 (level 7)

Metals are used for many items in modern life.

a Which two properties of copper make it useful for electrical wires? [2]

b Copper can be quarried as an ore or a native metal. Give one economic advantage of a new quarry opening in a community. [1]

c Give one environmental advantage of quarrying native copper instead of copper ore. [1]

d Explain why it is important to recycle metals like copper. [2]

Chemical Reactions

Chemical reactions

What is change?

The world around us is full of change. Some of these changes, such as the freezing of water into ice, are easily changed back or reversed. When no new substance is made, a physical change has happened. The particles change *how they are arranged*, but the substance does not change its chemical properties.

When charcoal is burned or combusted on a barbeque, the carbon from the fuel and oxygen from the air are changed. They turn into carbon dioxide. This is an example of a chemical reaction. In a chemical reaction a new substance is made. Most chemical reactions cannot be changed back under the same conditions and are called irreversible.

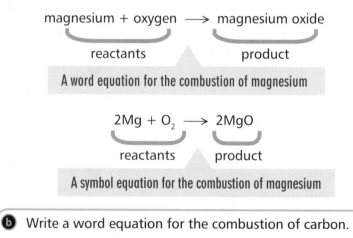

A barbeque shows a chemical reaction

A thermal spring in Yellowstone National Park. How many physical changes can you see in this picture?

a What is the difference between a chemical reaction and a physical change?

We can record chemical reactions in equations. The starting substances are called reactants. We show them on the left of the arrow. The new substances formed are called products and are written on the right of the arrow. The arrow means that the reactants 'go to' the products.

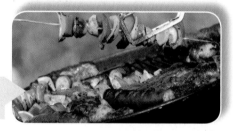

$$\text{magnesium} + \text{oxygen} \longrightarrow \text{magnesium oxide}$$

reactants   product

A word equation for the combustion of magnesium

$$2Mg + O_2 \longrightarrow 2MgO$$

reactants   product

A symbol equation for the combustion of magnesium

Did You Know?

Nitrogen from the air can react with hydrogen to make ammonia; this is a chemical reaction called the Haber Process. However, the ammonia that is produced breaks down to make nitrogen and hydrogen again. This is a reversible reaction. Eventually, the amounts of hydrogen, nitrogen and ammonia stay constant, even though both the reactions are still happening.

b Write a word equation for the combustion of carbon.

Classifying changes

It is important for scientists to be able to sort or classify their observations. This makes it easier to explain their findings to other scientists and to make predictions for other changes that they plan to study.

You are going to study three changes. You should decide if the changes are chemical, physical, reversible or irreversible. Copy the results table below before you start your experiments. You should put a tick in two columns per change to classify your change.

Change	Chemical change	Physical change	Reversible	Irreversible
Sodium chloride + ice				
Magnesium + hydrochloric acid				
Warming iodine				

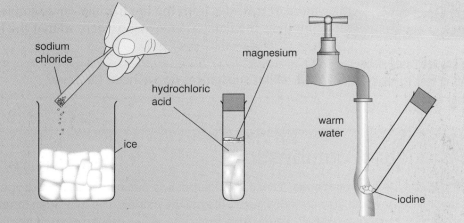

- Add 2–3 spatulas of sodium chloride (salt) to ice.
- Add a piece of magnesium to half a test tube of hydrochloric acid.

  ▷ **Safety:** Wear eye protection.

- Your teacher will give you a sealed test tube with a few crystals of iodine in the bottom. Hold the end of the test tube under warm running water, observe. Remove the test tube from the warm water and observe until the test tube has cooled back to room temperature.

  ▷ **Safety:** Do not remove the bung.

Combustion

C2.2

- ▶▶ What is combustion?
- ▶▶ What are the products of combustion of wax?

Combustion has been used since ancient times to keep humans warm and cook food

A burning question

Combustion is the word we use in science for 'burning'. In burning, **oxides** are formed. Oxygen gas is needed for the new oxides to be made. So, combustion is a type of chemical reaction.

A fire needs fuel, oxygen and heat. If any one of these is missing then the combustion reaction will stop. There are many ways to put out a fire; all of them remove one or more of the sides from the fire triangle. For example, a fire blanket smothers the flames, removing oxygen, so that the fire goes out.

The fire triangle

ⓐ What substances do we need for a fire?

Products of combustion

Many fuels are **hydrocarbons**. These are compounds that contain only hydrogen and carbon atoms. When they are combusted they make oxides. The hydrogen turns into an oxide of hydrogen (water). The carbon turns into either carbon dioxide or carbon monoxide, depending on how much oxygen is present. You are going to investigate the products of combustion of a hydrocarbon, wax.

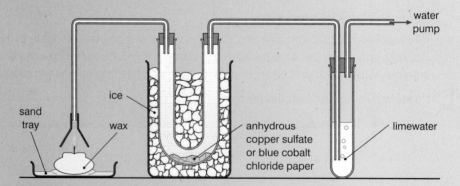

sand tray · wax · ice · anhydrous copper sulfate or blue cobalt chloride paper · limewater · water pump

A candle is made out of wax, a type of hydrocarbon. Predict the products that will be made. Don't forget to use **scientific** ideas to explain your prediction.

- Your teacher is going to light the candle. Note down your observations.
- How were the products of combustion collected and tested?
- Write a word equation to summarise the chemical reaction that is happening.

We can use equations to summarise combustion reactions. The general equation for combustion is:

substance + oxygen ⟶ substance oxide

For hydrocarbons this general equation becomes:

hydrocarbon + oxygen ⟶ water + carbon dioxide

b Write a word equation for the combustion of methane (a type of hydrocarbon).

Which is complete and which is incomplete combustion?

Summary Questions

1 Copy and complete the passage using the words below:

hydrocarbons   chemical   water   fuels   triangle

Combustion is a type of … reaction. … are substances that are burned to release energy in a more useable form. Many fuels are … They combust to produce an oxide of hydrogen, … , and oxides of carbon. The fire … tells us that fuel, oxygen and heat are all needed for a fire or a combustion reaction to happen.

2 Copy and complete the following word equations:

a)   magnesium +… ⟶ magnesium oxide

b)   petrol + oxygen ⟶ water + …

c)   … + oxygen ⟶ water + carbon dioxide

3 Carbon monoxide is a poisonous, odourless gas that can be made in faulty gas appliances in the home. Make a poster to explain why it is important to get your gas appliances checked regularly. Don't forget to include how carbon monoxide poisons you.

KEY WORDS

combustion
hydrocarbon

Energy from Fuels

▶▶ What is a fuel?

▶▶ How can I compare the energy content of fuels?

Fuel the fire

A **fuel** is a chemical that is combusted to release its stored energy in a more useable form, often as heat. Some fuels like coal and oil are **non-renewable**. They were formed underground over millions of years. This means that once they are used, it will take the Earth millions of years to make more, so they will run out. Other fuels such as wood and biomass are **renewable**. This means that they will not run out.

Many fuels are non-renewable

a What is the difference between renewable and non-renewable fuels?

Different fuels contain different amounts of energy per kilogram, depending on what molecules they are made of. It is important to pick the right fuel for the job. Most cars run on liquid fuels like petrol or diesel from crude oil. But you could use another liquid fuel, ethanol (alcohol), which is renewable. Liquid fuels have enough chemical energy locked up inside them to power the car, without being too heavy for the car to carry. As they are liquids they are easy to store and in a crash they are less likely to explode than a gas fuel.

b Give an example of a fuel for a car that is renewable.

Did You Know?

Many of the fuels that we use in the developed world are non-renewable fossil fuels. Fossil fuels are oil, coal and gas. They were made from dead plants and animals millions of years ago and they have been trapped beneath the Earth's surface without oxygen. Instead of rotting away, they have changed chemically into different hydrocarbons that we can use today as fuels and to make chemicals like plastics.

Brazilians use ethanol as a fuel in their cars

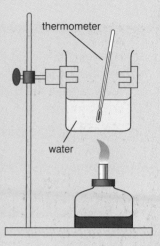

Which fuel can provide most energy?

Fuels can be solids, liquids or gases. You are going to investigate how much chemical energy is locked in three different liquid fuels.

- Put 150 cm³ of water into a 250 cm³ beaker and clamp into place.
- Take the starting temperature of the water.
- Measure the starting mass of the spirit burner and the fuel.
- Light the spirit burner and put it under the beaker.
- Take the temperature of the water every 30 seconds for 5 minutes, then blow the spirit burner out.
- Measure the final mass of the spirit burner and the fuel.
- Record your results in a table.
- Repeat the experiment with two other fuels.
- Calculate the amount of energy in one gram of the fuel.
- Write the names of the fuels from the most to the least amount of energy per gram.
- Explain how you made this experiment a fair test.

Safety: Be careful not to burn yourself on the flame or hot surfaces. Wear eye protection.

Stretch Yourself

Reliable results are similar every time you repeat the experiment. How can you make your results more reliable?

Accurate results are close to the true values. Do you think your results are accurate? Explain your answer.

Summary Questions

1 Match the key word to the correct definition:

a) Fuel	A natural resource that will run out.
b) Renewable	A natural resource that will not run out.
c) Non-renewable	A substance that is combusted to release its stored energy in a more useable form, often as heat.

2 Many different fuels were used in Scotland in 2002. 18% coal, 28% oil, 34% natural gas, 3% renewable and 17% nuclear fuel.
   a) Draw a pie chart of this data.
   b) What can you conclude from this data?

3 Make a table to show the fuels that you use at home and what they are used for.

What's the Damage? (2)

>> How might combustion of fuels damage the environment?

>> What is the difference between the greenhouse effect and global warming?

Greenhouse gases and global warming

Carbon dioxide, methane and water vapour in our atmosphere trap some of the reflected heat from the surface of the Earth. This natural process is called the **greenhouse effect** and causes the average world temperature to be high enough to support life as we know it.

a What are the three greenhouse gases?

The amount of carbon dioxide in the air is increasing. Many scientists believe that burning fossil fuels is to blame and it is causing **global warming**. Global warming is the increase in average world temperatures.

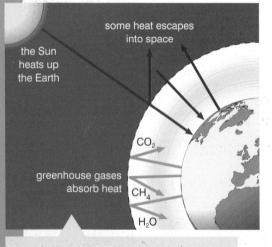

the Sun heats up the Earth

some heat escapes into space

CO_2

greenhouse gases absorb heat CH_4

H_2O

The greenhouse effect is a natural process

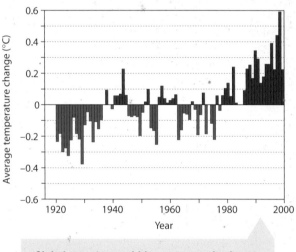

Global warming could be a man-made change

There are many predictions about global warming. The ice caps could melt, sea levels would rise and low lying areas would flood. Climate could change and farmers would have to grow different crops. Diseases such as malaria may increase.

Did You Know?

Scientists study ice cores from the Arctic to give information about how the atmosphere has changed over time. Some scientists believe that global warming is actually part of the Earth's natural heating and cooling pattern but most agree it is more likely to be caused by human activity.

Acid rain

Many fossil fuels have impurities containing sulfur in them. When the fuels are combusted, the sulfur is turned into sulfur dioxide. In the heat of a car engine, nitrogen from the air can react to form nitrogen oxides. These gases from fuel combustion and car engines mix with rain water and cause acid rain.

b Which gases cause acid rain?

Acid rain pollutes lakes and soil. This changes the animals and plants that can live in that environment. Acid rain can be prevented by removing the sulfur impurities before we burn the fuel or by using gas scrubbers to neutralise the acidic waste gases from chimneys. Catalytic converters on cars remove the nitrogen oxides from waste exhaust gases.

activity

Effects of carbon dioxide and methane on temperature

There is a mixture of different gases in the atmosphere. Some of these gases trap heat energy from the Sun and this acts like a blanket around the Earth to keep it warm. You are going to investigate the effect of different gases on the temperature of a sealed container.

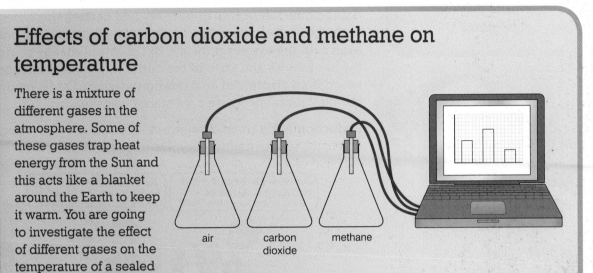

air   carbon dioxide   methane

- Put a temperature probe through a hole in a bung.
- Push the bung into the top of a conical flask with air in it.
- Put another temperature probe into a conical flask of carbon dioxide and a third into a conical flask of methane.
- Place the three flasks on the window ledge and set the computer to collect the data.
- Make a prediction about what you think will happen – don't forget to use science to explain your ideas.
- After half an hour, take a look at your results. Was your prediction correct? How could this information be used to explain how humans could be causing global warming?

Summary Questions

1 Match the correct endings to the following sentences:

a) Global warming	and nitrogen oxidising in car engines.
b) The greenhouse effect	could be a man-made effect.
c) Acid rain is caused by sulfur impurities in fossil fuels	is a natural process.
d) Acid rain can be prevented by using a gas scrubber,	catalytic converter or removing sulfur before the fuel is combusted.

2 Make a poster to explain the difference between global warming and the greenhouse effect.

KEY WORDS

carbon dioxide
greenhouse effect
global warming
acid rain

Oxidation

➤ What is oxidation?

➤ What is the product of oxidation?

Rancid butter is an example of an oxidation reaction

Next time you...

... have a half full plastic bottle of oil, look carefully at the container. The fat molecules react with the oxygen in the air inside the closed bottle. The oxidation reaction reduces the air pressure in the bottle, but the atmospheric pressure on the outside of the bottle stays the same. This means that the bottle will be pushed inwards and so you should be able to see it starting to look crushed.

Spacecraft like Apollo 11 have to take their own oxygen supply for combustion in the engines

Reacting with oxygen

When you leave a packet of butter open in the kitchen, have you noticed how the surface goes crusty and darker? This is described as the butter becoming **rancid**. The fat molecules in the butter react with the oxygen in the air. This chemical change causes the appearance and taste of the butter to change. Butter going rancid is an example of an **oxidation** reaction. Oxidation describes chemical reactions where a substance gains oxygen.

Reduction is the chemical opposite of oxidation. In a reduction reaction a substance loses oxygen.

a Is oxidation a chemical or physical change? Explain your answer.

Combustion is one of the most common oxidation reactions. Combustion can happen even when there is no oxygen gas. Oxygen in the form of liquid or solid, like in a space rocket, can also be used for oxidation.

Some chemicals like hydrogen peroxide (H_2O_2) have oxygen locked up inside them, which can be used in a combustion reaction. These chemicals are called **oxidising agents**. They should be stored carefully to prevent accidental combustion reactions.

CORROSIVE
These substances attack and destroy living tissues, including eyes and skin

IRRITANT
These substances are not corrosive but can cause reddening or blistering of the skin

OXIDISING
These substances provide oxygen, which allows other materials to burn more fiercely

HARMFUL
These substances are similar to toxic substances but less dangerous.

HIGHLY FLAMMABLE
These substances catch fire easily

TOXIC
These substances can cause death. They may have their poisonous effects when swallowed, or breathed in, or absorbed through the skin

Oxidisers have their own hazard symbol

b Give an example of an oxidising agent.

activity

Oxidation

Vinegar is a weak acid. Alcohol like wine can be oxidised to vinegar when it is left open to the air. You are going to investigate the pH of different drinks when they have been freshly opened and when they have been oxidised.

- In a dimple dish put a sample of white wine, red wine, sherry, white wine vinegar, red wine vinegar and sherry vinegar.

- Using a pH probe or universal indicator paper test the pH of each liquid.

- Record you results in a table.

- What conclusions can you draw from this experiment?

Stretch Yourself

If one chemical is oxidised and gains oxygen, another chemical will lose oxygen. The chemical that loses oxygen is reduced. Oxidation and reduction happen at the same time, and so the overall reaction is described as a REDOX reaction. Can you think of any examples of redox reactions?

Summary Questions

1 Match the key word to the correct definition:

a) Rancid	A chemical reaction where a substance gains oxygen.
b) Oxidation	Describes product when fat is oxidised.
c) Reduction	A substance that contains a lot of oxygen that it can give up in a chemical reaction.
d) Oxidising agent	A chemical reaction where a substance loses oxygen.

2 Complete the following oxidation reactions:

a) ... + oxygen $\longrightarrow$ iron oxide

b) carbon + oxygen $\longrightarrow$ ...

c) ethanol + ... $\longrightarrow$ water + carbon dioxide

3 The definition of oxidation and reduction can be extended. Write a revision book article to explain what oxidation and reduction are and don't forget to include examples.

KEY WORDS

rancid
oxidation
reduction
oxidising agent

Acid and Metal Carbonates

▶▶ What happens when an acid reacts with a metal carbonate?

▶▶ Do all metal carbonates react and make similar products?

The White Cliffs of Dover are made from chalk

✚ Help Yourself

Think back to Fusion Book 1. How can you test for carbon dioxide gas using limewater?

science@work

Metal carbonates have many uses in the food industry. Sodium carbonate is also known as E500 and is used as an acidity regulator, anti-caking agent, raising agent and stabiliser. Calcium carbonate is often added to soya milk to increase the calcium needed for strong bones and teeth. Magnesium carbonate is used to help foods keep their colour.

**S: Wheat Flour, Water, Vegeta
sing Agents (E450, E500, E34
ilycerine), Acidity Regulators (
id), Emulsifier (E471), Preser
Flour Treatment Agent (E92**

Metal carbonates

Limestone, marble and chalk are mainly made from calcium **carbonate**. This is an example of a metal carbonate. Metal carbonates are **bases**. Bases will neutralise acids in a chemical reaction. The chemical reaction will always make a metal salt, **carbon dioxide** and water.

activity

Metal carbonates and acids

Chemical weathering can happen when metal carbonates in rocks react with acid in rain water. This chemical reaction can be speeded up with acid rain (look back to pages 84–85 to remind yourself about acid rain). You are going to investigate which rocks would be affected and which metal carbonate they contain.

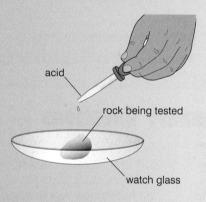

acid

rock being tested

watch glass

- Collect samples of different rocks.
- Put one of the samples in the centre of a watch glass.
- Using a dropping pipette, add a few drops of sulfuric acid onto the rock. Make your observations.
- Wash the rock and add a few drops of nitric acid. Make your observations.
- Wash the rock and add a few drops of carbonic acid. Make your observations.
- Repeat with the other types of rock.
- Record your observations in a table.
- Explain why these three acids were chosen for this experiment.
- What can you conclude from this experiment?

▷ **Safety:** Wear gloves and eye protection.

ⓐ What is the liquid product made when a metal carbonate reacts with an acid?

The general equation for a metal carbonate reacting with an acid is:

metal carbonate + acid $\longrightarrow$ salt + water + carbon dioxide

ⓑ Complete this word equation:

… + hydrochloric acid $\longrightarrow$ calcium chloride + … + carbon dioxide

Did You Know?

Sherbet uses a neutralisation reaction between sodium carbonate and citric acid. These two dry chemicals do not react until the water (from saliva) in your mouth touches them. This causes carbon dioxide to be made and a fizzing sensation to be felt. A harmless salt of sodium citrate and water are also made.

Sherbet causes a cold fizzing in your mouth as a chemical reaction happens

Summary Questions

❶ Match the correct endings to the following sentences:

a)	Limestone, chalk and marble	can neutralise acids.
b)	Metal carbonates	to cloudy when carbon dioxide is passed into it.
c)	Limewater turns from colourless	all contain calcium carbonate.
d)	Acids react with metal carbonates to	produce water, metal salt and carbon dioxide.

❷ Copy and complete the following word equations:

a) Sodium carbonate + … $\longrightarrow$ sodium nitrate + carbon dioxide + water

b) … + hydrochloric acid $\longrightarrow$ copper chloride + … + water

c) Magnesium carbonate + sulfuric acid $\longrightarrow$ … + … + …

❸ When a piece of chalk is put into sulfuric acid it begins to undergo a chemical reaction in which insoluble calcium sulfate is formed. However, this reaction stops before all the acid or all the calcium carbonate has been used. Explain this observation.

KEY WORDS

carbonate
base
carbon dioxide

Making Salts

> ▶▶ What is the difference between an acid and a base?
>
> ▶▶ What is neutralisation?
>
> ▶▶ How can we plan to make a salt?

Let's neutralise!

Bacteria in your mouth feed on sugar. They make **acid** which attacks your teeth. However, we can prevent tooth decay by using toothpaste which contains a weak **base** like calcium carbonate. A chemical reaction called **neutralisation** happens between the acid in your mouth and the basic calcium carbonate.

> **a** Why would you neutralise a bee sting with a weak alkali and not a strong alkali?

Bee stings contain acid

Bases

In a neutralisation reaction, a **salt** is always made. There are three general equations for neutralisation:

$$acid + alkali \longrightarrow salt + water$$

$$acid + metal\ carbonate \longrightarrow salt + water + carbon\ dioxide$$

$$acid + metal\ oxide \longrightarrow salt + water$$

A salt is a metal compound that can be made from an acid. When we replace the hydrogen in an acid with a metal, a salt has been made. Hydrochloric acid will make a metal chloride, sulfuric acid will make a metal sulfate and nitric acid will make a metal nitrate.

> **b** Complete the following word equation:
>
> hydrochloric acid + magnesium oxide $\longrightarrow$ ...

Did You Know?

Bases are the group of chemicals that neutralise acids. If a base can dissolve in water then it can also be called an **alkali**. All alkalis are bases but not all bases are alkalis!

You can use the pH scale to tell you how acidic or alkaline a substance is. The pH of a liquid can be found out using universal indicator. This mixture of dyes changes into 15 different colours to tell you the pH of the solution. Electricity can also be used to work out the pH of a solution. The pH probes can be hand-held monitors, like those used by water companies to check the pH of streams and rivers. We can connect other monitors to a computer and use them as a data-logger.

The universal indicator pH scale

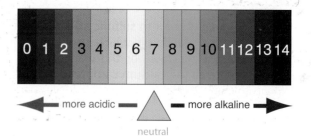

0 1 2 3 4 5 6 7 8 9 10 11 12 13 14

◀━ more acidic ━ △ ━ more alkaline ━▶

neutral

Investigating neutralisation

In the chemical industry it is important to think about all the different ways to make the substances that you are going to sell. After thinking about all the methods, the most efficient one, producing least waste, using the least energy and the most readily available starting materials should be chosen.

You are going to plan and make your own salt. Choose which salt you would like to make from the list below:

- Sodium chloride
- Copper sulfate
- Calcium nitrate

You must decide on your reactants (starting chemicals) and how you will make and separate the salt (think back to separating mixtures in Fusion Books 1 and 2). You should include a reason for choosing your method.

You can use any of the equipment found normally in a lab, but before you start you must write a risk assessment. Your risk assessment must include the hazards in your method, how you are going to reduce these and any emergency procedures that you would use. CLEAPSS hazcards help you complete this task.

Summary Questions

1 Copy and complete the passage using the words below:

salt   neutralisation   metal   hydrogen   acid

… is a chemical reaction that always makes a salt. Salts are compounds where the … in an acid has been changed for a metal. There are three main ways to make a metal … . To make a salt, … can react with either an alkali, metal carbonate or … oxide.

2 Copy and complete the following word equations:

a)   … + potassium hydroxide ⟶ potassium sulfate + water

b)   nitric acid + … ⟶ calcium nitrate + … + carbon dioxide

c)   … + calcium oxide ⟶ calcium chloride + …

3 Find out what a wasp sting contains and how it could be treated at home.

KEY WORDS

acid
base
neutralisation
salt
alkali

Exothermic and Endothermic Reactions

- ▸▸ What is an exothermic change?
- ▸▸ What is an endothermic change?

What's the energy change?

Chemical reactions always have a change in **energy**. Combustion is an example of an **exothermic** reaction. Energy, in the form of heat, light and maybe sound, can be given out. If energy is taken in during the reaction, such as sherbet fizzing on your tongue, it is described as an **endothermic** reaction.

activity

Classifying reactions

Plaster of Paris setting is an example of an exothermic chemical change. In an art lesson in 2007, a student was making a cast of her hands, and poured too much Plaster of Paris in the mould. The chemical reaction was so exothermic that it caused her to have severe burns on her hands and she needed medical treatment. It is important to know whether a reaction is exothermic or endothermic so that you can be safe.

You are going to study three different changes. You need to decide if they are a chemical or physical change and if they are an exothermic or endothermic change. You should copy and complete the following table:

Reaction	Starting temperature (°C)	Final temperature (°C)	Exothermic or endothermic?	Chemical or physical change?

Experiment 1: In a polystyrene beaker add 10 cm³ of hydrochloric acid and record the starting temperature. Add 10 cm³ of sodium hydroxide and stir with the thermometer. Record the new temperature.

▷ **Safety:** Wear chemical splash proof goggles.

Experiment 2: In a clean polystyrene beaker add 25 cm³ of water and record the starting temperature. Add 3 spatulas of potassium nitrate and record the temperature after all of the solid has dissolved.

Experiment 3: In a clean polystyrene beaker add 10 cm³ of copper sulfate solution and record the starting temperature. Add a spatula of magnesium powder and swirl the beaker. Record the new temperature.

▷ **Safety:** Wear eye protection and wash your hands after the experiment.

stir with a thermometer

polystyrene beaker

a Give an example of an endothermic reaction.

Often the energy taken in or released by a reaction is worked out from the change in temperature. If the temperature of a reaction increases, then the reaction is exothermic; but if the temperature goes down the reaction is endothermic.

b In a chemical reaction, the temperature of the liquid increased by 1°C. Is this an exothermic or endothermic change? Explain your answer.

Exothermic
Heat 'exits' (is given *out*). The temperature outside goes up.

Fireworks are an example of an exothermic reaction

Evaporation of sea water is an example of an endothermic change

Endothermic
Heat 'enters' (is taken *in*). The temperature outside goes down.

Summary Questions

1 Match the key word to the correct definition:

a) Exothermic	A variable measured in joules (J). It cannot be created or destroyed, only changed from one form to another.
b) Endothermic	A change that takes in energy.
c) Energy	A change that gives out energy.

2 Syed recorded some results for two chemical reactions. His results are below:

Reaction	Starting temperature	Ending temperature (°C)
A	19	34
B	21	15

a) What has Syed missed from his results table?

b) Which reaction was exothermic?

c) Which reaction was endothermic?

3 Make a poster to explain the difference between exothermic and endothermic changes. On your poster include three examples of each type of change.

Link up to... HISTORY

Physical changes can also be exothermic or endothermic. The Victorians did not have freezers but they could make ice cream. They sprinkled salt onto ice; this caused an endothermic physical change to happen as the salt mixed with the water in the ice. The ice cream mixture was then stirred in a bowl over the salty ice and the cooling effect was used to freeze the ice cream.

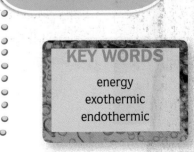

KEY WORDS

energy
exothermic
endothermic

Conservation of Mass

> ▶▶ Does mass change in a chemical reaction?
>
> ▶▶ What is an open and closed system?

My dad suffers from 'conservation of mass' ... his diets never seem to work

It's a theory ...

In a chemical reaction, atoms in the reactants are rearranged to form the products. No atoms are created or destroyed. This means that the mass of the reactants is the same as the mass of the products. This idea is known as the **Conservation of Mass**.

> **a** Complete the equation for the conservation of mass.
>
> mass of reactants = ...

The theory of conservation of mass can also be seen in a physical change. In a physical change, the arrangement of the particles in the substance change, but no atoms are created or destroyed. This means that the mass stays the same.

> **b** A nail was left in an open test tube of water and it began to rust. The mass of the nail, test tube and water increased. But in a similar test tube with a bung, the mass remained the same. Explain this observation.

activity

Conservation of mass

Antoine Lavoisier was the first scientist to prove the conservation of mass theory. In 1775 he completed an experiment that lasted for 288 hours, where he heated mercury to make mercury oxide. He carefully measured the masses of the reactants and products. You are going to use an electronic balance to prove the conservation of mass theory.

- Put a measuring cylinder onto the balance and zero the balance. Measure $20\,cm^3$ of magnesium sulfate ($MgSO_4$) and record the mass.

- Put a measuring cylinder onto the balance and zero the balance. Measure $20\,cm^3$ of barium chloride ($BaCl_2$), and record the mass.

- Put a $100\,cm^3$ beaker onto the balance and zero the balance. Mix the two solutions in the beaker until the chemical reaction to form magnesium chloride ($MgCl_2$) and barium sulfate ($BaSO_4$) is complete. Record the final mass of the beaker and the mixture.

- What can you conclude from this experiment?

> ⚠ **Safety:** Barium chloride is harmful; make sure that you wash your hands after the experiment. Wear eye protection.

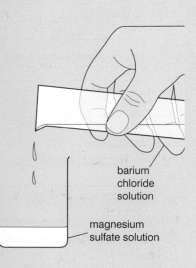

barium chloride solution

magnesium sulfate solution

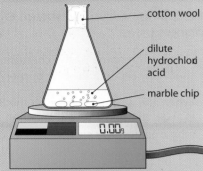

activity

Mass changes in a chemical reaction

You are going to investigate why some chemical reactions show mass changes. Your observations for both experiments should be recorded in the same results table.

cotton wool

dilute hydrochloric acid

marble chip

0.00ɡ

balance (reading to 0.01g)
(connected to computer if possible)

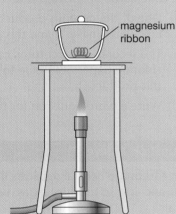

magnesium ribbon

Experiment 1

Measure 25 cm³ of hydrochloric acid into a conical flask. Weigh this on an electronic balance. Add a few pieces of marble. Wait a few minutes and then weigh it again. Explain your mass observations.

Experiment 2

Wind a 5–10 cm strip of magnesium ribbon into a coil and put it in a crucible with a lid. Record the starting mass. Using a Bunsen burner, tripod and pipe clay triangle, heat the crucible for 5 minutes lifting the lid slightly every minute. Allow the crucible to cool before measuring its mass again.

Explain your mass observations.

 Safety: Be careful not to burn yourself. Wear eye protection.

Summary Questions

1 Match the correct endings to the following sentences:

a) In a closed system	states that the mass of reactants equals the mass of the products.
b) The Theory of Conservation of Mass	mass remains the same throughout a chemical reaction.
c) In a chemical reaction no	the Theory of the Conservation of Mass.
d) Both chemical and physical changes follow	atoms are created or destroyed, they are just rearranged.

2 Find out more about Lavoisier's famous experiment to prove the conservation of mass theory. Use this information to write a magazine article.

Stretch Yourself

If a chemical reaction cannot lose any products or gain any reactants, the mass will stay the same throughout the change. This is known as a closed system. But, in some chemical reactions, products can be lost or reactants can be added. This means that the mass appears to change and is known as an open system.

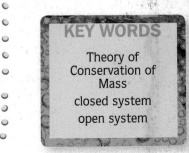

KEY WORDS

Theory of Conservation of Mass
closed system
open system

know your stuff

▼ Question 1 (level 4)

Annabel and Claire were looking at three different changes.

 a Which of the following changes was a chemical reaction?

burning match   ice cube melting   boiling water   [1]

 b Which gas is used as a match burns? Choose one of the following.

oxygen   carbon dioxide   hydrogen [1]

 c Which gas is made as a match burns? Choose one of the following.

oxygen   carbon dioxide   hydrogen [1]

 d Explain the difference between a chemical and physical change.   [2]

▼ Question 2 (level 5)

Litmus is an indicator. It is blue in alkaline solutions, purple in neutral solutions and red in acidic solutions.

a What happens when lemon juice is put on blue litmus paper?   [1]

b Hydrochloric acid can react with sodium hydroxide. Copy and complete the word equation for this reaction.

sodium hydroxide   ...
      +   ⟶   +
hydrochloric acid   ...   [1]

c What is the name of this type of chemical reaction?   [1]

d (i) What colour would you predict litmus paper to be if it was dipped into the products?   [1]

(ii) Explain your answer.   [1]

▼ Question 3 (level 6)

Bunsen burners are used in science to heat substances.

a What is the name of the chemical reaction that happens in a Bunsen burner?   [1]

b When the air hole is open in the Bunsen burner, the flame is at its hottest. Explain why opening the air hole makes the flame hotter.   [1]

c The fuel for a Bunsen burner is methane. In the blue flame only two products are made.

(i) One of the gaseous products turns limewater milky. Name this product. [1]

(ii) The second product turns cobalt chloride paper from blue to pink. Name this product.   [1]

(iii) Write a word equation for this reaction.

... + ... ⟶ ... + ...   [2]

▼ Question 4 (level 7)

Calcium carbonate neutralises acids like hydrochloric acid to produce a gas, water and a metal salt.

a Write a word equation for this reaction.   [3]

b Sally completed the reaction using the equipment shown below.

(i) What would you expect to happen to the mass reading?   [1]

(ii) Explain your answer.   [2]

How Science Works

▼ Question 1 (level 4)

André combusted magnesium ribbon in a crucible and measured the mass of the empty crucible, the crucible at the start of the reaction and at the end of the reaction.

a What would the unit of mass be? Choose one of the following.

N   s   g   [1]

b Name the equipment that André would use to measure the mass.   [1]

c Why did the crucible gain mass at the end of the reaction?   [2]

▼ Question 2 (level 5)

Muntaz decided that she would investigate the reaction between calcium carbonate and hydrochloric acid. She monitored the temperature of the solution to see how it changed.

a Put the following statements in order to show the method that Muntaz would have used.

Measure 5 g of calcium carbonate and put this into the acid.

Measure the temperature of the mixture every 30 seconds for 10 minutes.

Put a thermometer into the acid and record the starting temperature.

Measure 25 cm³ of hydrochloric acid into a conical flask.   [2]

b What hazard symbol would be shown on the bottle of hydrochloric acid?   [1]

c Muntaz recorded her information in a table and then drew a line graph.

(i) What would be the variable on the x-axis?   [1]

(ii) What would be the unit of the variable on the y-axis?   [1]

d How could Muntaz check if her results were accurate?   [1]

▼ Question 3 (level 6)

Isaac decided to find out how much energy was stored in methanol, ethanol and propanol. He burned 1 g of the fuel and used the energy given out to heat 50 cm³ of water. He noted the temperature change in the water, to the nearest 1°C.

a Draw a results table for Isaac to record his data.   [6]

b How could Isaac make his results more precise?   [1]

c Isaac found that his results were reliable but not accurate. Explain how this could be the case.   [2]

▼ Question 4 (level 7)

The average world temperatures and the amount of carbon dioxide in the atmosphere have been studied and the data put onto the following line graph:

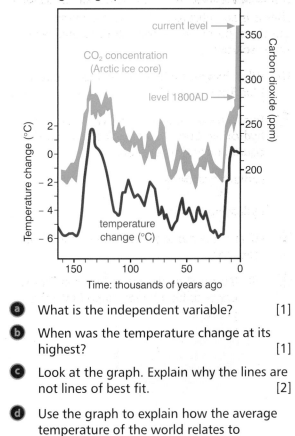

a What is the independent variable?   [1]

b When was the temperature change at its highest?   [1]

c Look at the graph. Explain why the lines are not lines of best fit.   [2]

d Use the graph to explain how the average temperature of the world relates to the amount of carbon dioxide in the atmosphere.   [2]

Energy and Electricity

Energy and electricity

Human energy

Human beings need energy to do things. We get the energy we use from our food.

In fact, our bodies use energy even when we are doing nothing. Our brains are big energy consumers – they use almost half of our body's energy supply:

- Energy used by an average human being while resting is 100 joules each second.
- Energy used by an average human brain while doing nothing is 40 joules each second.

If you are active, for example when you are doing sport, your body uses energy much more quickly.

In developed countries, such as the UK, we use much more energy than the energy we gain from our food – roughly ten times as much.

Basketball is an energetic sport – especially if you have to move around in a wheelchair

- We use energy for travelling around.
- We use energy for heating our homes and other buildings.
- We use energy to make things and to entertain us.

That's what it means to live in a developed nation. We have lots of machines, busy using energy, doing useful things for us.

> **a** List some machines you have made use of today. What did you use them for? Where did they get their supply of energy from?

These industrial robots are building a car – saving human energy

Energy along the wires

Electricity is a good way of transferring energy from place to place. Electric current in wires and cables carries energy from power stations to where we want to use it.

Most of the electricity we use is produced by burning fossil fuels: coal, gas and oil. But we are making more and more use of other ways of generating electricity, from the energy of the wind, for example.

> **b** Where have you seen cables carrying electricity in your neighbourhood?

Energy landscape

To generate electricity, we must start with an energy resource. Then we need a way to convert the energy into electricity. For example, sunlight is an energy resource; solar cells (photovoltaic cells) transfer the energy of sunlight using electrical energy to do work.

Look at the picture of the landscape. If you had lived ten thousand years ago, you would have seen plants and animals as the main energy resources in the landscape. In the 21st century, we have the technology to make use of many more of the energy resources around us.

In this topic, you will learn about how electricity is generated and how we use it to deliver energy in several different ways.

---

activity

We have the technology ...

Work with a partner to discuss the different energy resources in the landscape shown in the picture. Can you think of any other useful energy resources?

How can we use each energy resource to generate electricity?

Make a poster showing a landscape in which electricity is being generated from different energy resources – include as many as you can. Label your poster to explain what is going on.

Energy in Store

▶▶ What is kinetic
energy?

▶▶ What forms of stored
energy are there?

Get moving

A moving object has energy. This is **kinetic energy**, also known as KE. For example, the wind is moving air, so it has KE.

You can see when an object is moving, so it seems obvious that it has energy. But there are other objects which have energy that is not so obvious. Here is an example:

It takes energy to climb up to the high diving board. Gravity is trying to pull you downwards, so you have to use energy to get higher.

When you stand on the board, you are a store of energy. Step out into space and you plunge downwards, going faster and faster, until you hit the water with a terrific splash.

The energy you store at the top of the dive is called **gravitational potential energy**, also known as GPE. 'Potential' is another way of saying 'stored' and it is 'gravitational' because you have worked against gravity to store the energy.

Any object which is high up has GPE:

- a hammer lifted up, ready to strike a nail,
- a skier at the top of the ski run,
- water behind the dam of a reservoir,
- a satellite in orbit around the Earth.

On your marks... sprinter without kinetic energy

Go... sprinter with kinetic energy

ⓐ Think of two more examples of objects which are stores of GPE. Explain how you know they have GPE.

ⓑ Give an example of something which has both KE and GPE. Explain how you know it has both forms of energy.

Next time you...

... climb the stairs, think about your GPE increasing.

I've got more GPE than you!

But I won't bump my head on the bottom of the pool!

More stores

There are other stores of potential energy:

- A stretched rubber band or a wound-up spring is a store of **elastic potential energy**. Release it and it can make something move.
- Chemical substances are stores of **chemical potential energy**. When the chemicals react, their stored energy is released. We make use of this when we burn fuels such as wood, gas or petrol. Batteries contain chemicals which react to make a current flow.
- Nuclear fuels such as uranium are also energy stores. They can lie in the ground for millions of years without giving up any of their energy. Put them in a nuclear power station and they can be made to release their energy at a controlled rate.

This clockwork radio has a wound-up spring inside. Switch on and the spring slowly unwinds, turning a generator to make electricity. (It also has solar cells.)

c How is energy stored in food?

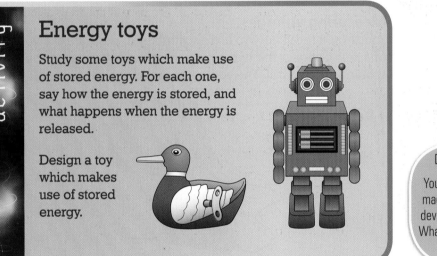

activity

Energy toys

Study some toys which make use of stored energy. For each one, say how the energy is stored, and what happens when the energy is released.

Design a toy which makes use of stored energy.

Link up to...

DESIGN AND TECHNOLOGY

You have probably designed and made toys and other interesting devices in design and technology. What energy stores did you make use of?

Summary Questions

1 What kind of energy store does a moving train have?

2 How is energy stored by a roller coaster car at the top of its ride, before it sets off?

3 A clock needs energy to make it work. Different clocks use different energy stores. Describe how a clock can make use of:
   a) elastic potential energy,
   b) chemical energy,
   c) gravitational potential energy.

4 Bungee jumpers start off high up. When they jump, they speed up as they fall. Then they stretch the elastic rope which they are attached to. What energy changes are happening?

KEY WORDS

kinetic energy
potential energy
gravitational potential energy
elastic potential energy
chemical potential energy

Electricity from Chemicals

▶▶ How can we use cells to provide different voltages?

▶▶ What's inside an electrical cell?

Providing the push

An electric circuit needs something to make a current flow. Cells, batteries, **power supplies**, the electrical mains – these all provide the push needed to get a current flowing around a circuit.

The voltage of a cell tells you about its push. The bigger the voltage, the stronger the push and so the greater the current will be:

- A single cell might provide 1.2 V, 1.5 V or 2.0 V.
- To provide a bigger voltage, connect two or more cells together in series (end-to-end) to make a battery.
- A power supply can give you different voltages, perhaps up to 12 V.
- Mains electricity has a voltage of 230 V. That can make a big current flow, so we must use it with great care.

Measuring voltages

You should recall how to use a voltmeter to measure the voltage of a cell. Connect the two **terminals** of the voltmeter to the two terminals of the cell. The voltmeter shows the voltage.

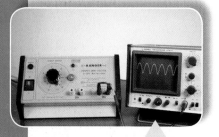

Turning the knob on this power supply changes the voltage between 0 V and 12 V

(a) Draw a circuit diagram to show how to measure the voltage of a cell.

Did You Know?

Batteries can be an expensive way to supply electricity. If you bought non-rechargeable batteries to power your home, your bill would be about 1000 times as much!

Next time you ...

... put new batteries in an appliance, work out their combined voltage.

activity

One (volt) plus one (volt) makes ... ?

Most torches use two or more cells. They are connected in series. A single cell would give a very dim light because the voltage would be small.

- If you connect two or more cells in series, what voltage do you get? What is the rule?
- Discuss the rule with your partner and devise a way to test it. You can use several cells, a voltmeter and connecting wires.

What's in a cell?

All cells contain chemicals. Some of these chemicals are highly poisonous – that's why it is **hazardous** to open up a cell or battery.

The chemicals inside a cell are a store of chemical potential energy. When a cell is connected in a complete circuit, the chemicals inside it start to react together. This releases their stored energy and the current carries the energy round the circuit to the different components.

Eventually, all of the chemicals will have reacted and the cell no longer stores energy. Used cells should always be disposed of with care.

> **b** How can you dispose of a used cell or battery so that the chemicals inside do not harm the environment?

activity

Locked in a cell

- Your teacher will show you the chemicals inside one or more cells.

- You can also see how to make a cell using dilute acid and two pieces of metal.

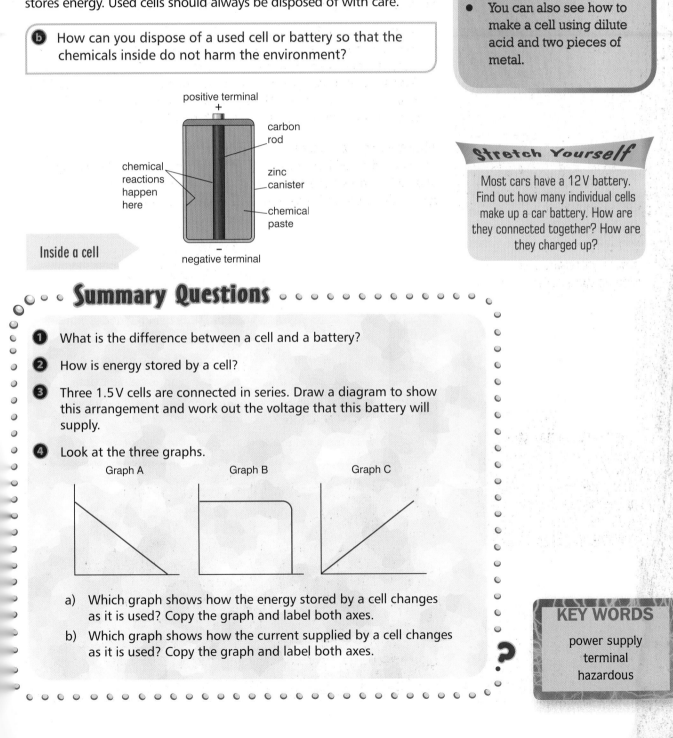

positive terminal
+

carbon rod

chemical reactions happen here

zinc canister

chemical paste

–
negative terminal

Inside a cell

Stretch Yourself

Most cars have a 12 V battery. Find out how many individual cells make up a car battery. How are they connected together? How are they charged up?

Summary Questions

1 What is the difference between a cell and a battery?

2 How is energy stored by a cell?

3 Three 1.5 V cells are connected in series. Draw a diagram to show this arrangement and work out the voltage that this battery will supply.

4 Look at the three graphs.

Graph A   Graph B   Graph C

a) Which graph shows how the energy stored by a cell changes as it is used? Copy the graph and label both axes.

b) Which graph shows how the current supplied by a cell changes as it is used? Copy the graph and label both axes.

KEY WORDS

power supply
terminal
hazardous

Electricity from Movement

▶▶ How can we generate electricity from movement?

▶▶ What energy changes happen in a wind turbine?

Well I'm blowed

Wind turbines come in different sizes. You may see a small one on a house or caravan. Big ones can dominate the landscape – their towers may be 200 m high.

a Where have you seen wind turbines? How big were they?

Behind the turbine

When you look at a wind turbine, you notice the long blades which spin when the wind blows. These make up the **turbine**.

But how does this generate electricity? At the back, behind the turbine, is a **generator**. A rotating shaft from the turbine makes the generator spin and this produces electricity. Thick cables (wires) carry the electric current to the foot of the turbine tower, where it joins the mains electricity grid.

b How does a rotating shaft store energy?

This visitor centre makes its own electricity using a wind turbine

Here you can see an engineer working on a new wind turbine. The generator is housed in the cylindrical blue box at the back, behind the turbine

activity

Turbine testing

You can investigate wind turbines using a model wind power kit:

- The generator is housed in a plastic container.
- You can fit different turbine blades on the front.
- Use a fan to create the wind which will make your turbine turn.
- Use a voltmeter to measure the voltage produced.

Link up to...

GEOGRAPHY

What makes a good site for a wind turbine? Where are the best areas in the UK for siting wind farms?

Energy changes

The wind is moving air. It has kinetic energy. When the wind causes a wind turbine to spin, some of its KE is transferred to the blades of the turbine.

The turbine causes the generator to turn and this produces electrical energy. The **electrical energy** is carried away by the current.

activity

Investigating wind power

Once you have found out how to make a model wind turbine, you can investigate it. How can you increase the voltage it produces?

- You could fit different turbines on the front of the generator.
- You could try altering the size, shape and angle of the turbine blades.
- You could try changing the wind speed – but how will you measure this?

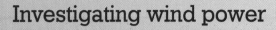

Great Debates

Wind power is a controversial way to generate electricity. While it is the most tested of all renewable sources and does not produce greenhouse gases, many people feel that wind turbines spoil the landscape and are noisy when you get close to them. Should we find other ways of generating electricity?

Imagine that a power company has approached your school as a site for three new wind turbines. They are willing to pay £2000 per month to the school. What are the arguments for and against the idea? What is your view?

'The fan blows the turbine round to generate the electricity to turn the fan – but somehow it doesn't work!'

Summary Questions

1 What is being described here?
   a) a series of blades which are forced to rotate when the wind blows
   b) an electrical device which, when forced to rotate, produces electricity.

2 Draw a diagram to show the energy changes which happen when a wind turbine produces electricity.

3 Find out about some real wind turbines. How big are they? How fast do they spin? How much do they contribute to the electricity supply?

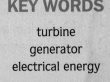

KEY WORDS

turbine
generator
electrical energy

Electricity from Fuels

▶▶ How can we generate
electricity from fuels?

▶▶ What happens to all
the energy?

This large power station uses
natural gas as its fuel

Burning questions

Most of the electricity we use comes from large power stations, not
from wind turbines. These power stations mostly use gas or coal as
their **fuel**.

A large power station may produce enough electricity for a city of
one million people. It will require a trainload of coal every hour to
keep it running.

> **a** Give at least four examples of fuels.

Looking inside
What happens inside a power station?

- The burning fuel heats water in a boiler. This produces high-
  pressure steam.
- The steam travels along pipes to a turbine.
- The steam pushes on the blades of the turbine, causing it to spin.
- The turbine forces a generator to turn, so that it generates
  electricity.

> **b** In what way is a power station similar to a wind turbine?
> In what way does it differ?

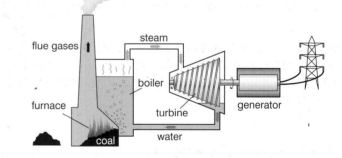

Help Yourself

*Look back through the earlier pages of
this topic. Make a list of all the different
forms of energy which have been
mentioned.*

activity

Inside out

Look at an animation of a power station. Look for:

- the furnace where the fuel is burned
- the boiler and the steam pipes
- the turbine and the generator.

How does electricity leave the power station?

If you have more than one animation to look at, compare
different types of power station.

Energy changes in a power station

Fuels are stores of chemical energy. When they burn, they react with oxygen in the air to release their stored energy. The energy released spreads out – this is **heat energy**.

As with a wind turbine, the spinning turbine has kinetic energy. The generator produces electrical energy which is carried away by the electric current.

chemical energy stored in fuel	→	heat energy released by burning fuel	→	kinetic energy of spinning turbine	→	electrical energy carried away by current

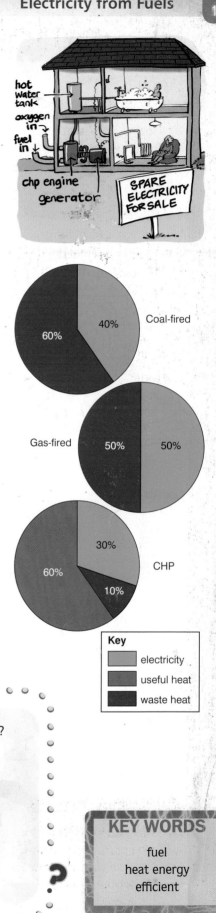

Making more of energy

Power stations use a lot of fuel but, unfortunately, much of the energy stored in the fuel is wasted. This is because a turbine can only extract a fraction of the energy carried by hot steam. The most **efficient** power stations waste about 50% of their energy supply. Others waste as much as 70%.

> **C** If a power station makes good use of 40% of the energy supplied to it, what percentage is wasted?

Some energy-efficient houses have a system which uses fuel to do two jobs:

- When the fuel burns, some of the heat released is used to generate electricity.
- The rest of the heat is used to produce hot water, or to heat the house.

This is called a combined heat and power (CHP) system. Only a small fraction of the energy of the fuel is wasted. A large CHP power station can supply electricity and hot water to hundreds of homes and offices.

Coal-fired: 40% / 60%

Gas-fired: 50% / 50%

CHP: 30% / 10% / 60%

Key
- electricity
- useful heat
- waste heat

Summary Questions

1. When a fuel burns, it needs a substance from the air. What substance?

2. Many modern power stations burn gas to generate electricity. The burning gas heats water in a boiler.
   a) How does the energy released by the burning gas reach the turbine?
   b) When the turbine spins, how does this produce electricity?

3. The pie charts show how three different power stations make use of the energy supplied to them by their fuels. Which is the most efficient and which is the least efficient?

KEY WORDS

fuel
heat energy
efficient

From Electricity to Heat

▸▸ How can we heat things with electricity?

▸▸ What is electrical resistance?

I knew that electric heater was a bad idea.

Did You Know?

The filament of en electric lamp may reach temperatures as high as 3000°C when switched on. The glass only gets to 500°C.

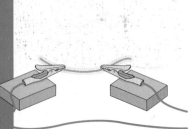

Warming up

There are many ways in which we use electricity. For example, we can use electricity to heat things up:

- Electric heaters get hot when they are switched on.
- Electric hotplates and ovens also use electricity to produce heat.
- An electric immersion heater heats water in the hot water tank.
- The rear windscreen of a car is heated electrically to remove frost and condensation.

All of these make use of the **heating effect** of an electric current.

> **a** Name some more electrical appliances that use electricity to produce heat.

activity

Hot stuff

Watch as your teacher connects a metal wire [or wire wool] to a power supply.

As the voltage increases, a current starts to flow through the metal.

The metal starts to glow.

The bigger the voltage, the bigger the current. A bigger current gives a bigger heating effect. The metal glows more brightly.

Heating effect

When an electric current flows through a metal wire, the wire may get hot. Some of the energy carried by the current is transferred to the wire.

- An electric heater has wires which get hot, but not too hot, when it is connected to the mains.
- A traditional light bulb has a filament which gets very hot, over 1000°C, when the current flows through it. This gives light as well as heat.

> **b** A light bulb gets hot when in use. Why is this a waste of energy?

activity

Water heater

In the lab, you can use a small low voltage electrical heater to heat some water. (The heating wires are surrounded by insulation so that the electric current does not come into contact with the water.)

- Use an ammeter to measure the current flowing through the heater.
- Use a thermometer to monitor the temperature of the water.

This thermogram of an electric heater shows how it gets hot when an electric current flows through it

What's going on?

Why does an electric current have a heating effect as it flows though a wire?

An electric current carries energy. It cannot flow completely freely through a wire, because the wire has electrical **resistance**. It gives up some of its energy in overcoming this resistance. The energy it loses makes the wire get hotter.

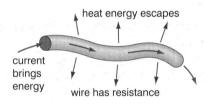

heat energy escapes

current brings energy

wire has resistance

Here's another way to think of this:

A current is a flow of **electrons** in a metal wire. Electrons are tiny particles that carry energy. As they move through the metal, they bump into the atoms of the metal. This slows them down so that they lose some of their energy to the atoms. The electrons lose energy and the atoms gain energy – the metal gets hotter.

An electrical water heater

science @ work

Scientists have learned how to control the movement of electrons so that we can use them to do all sorts of useful things – that's the work of electrical and electronic engineers.

Summary Questions

1. What happens to the temperature of a wire when an electric current flows through it?

2. State three ways in which we can make use of the heating effect of an electric current.

3. A student says, 'When a current flows through a wire, it loses some of its energy. This means less current comes out of the other end of the wire'.

   Do you agree? Explain your answer, and describe how you would test your idea with an experiment.

KEY WORDS

heating effect
resistance
electron

Paying the Price

▶▶ How can we measure electrical energy?

▶▶ How do we pay for electricity?

Energy meter

Electricity is a useful way of transferring energy from place to place. That's why we make so much use of it. But we have to pay for it!

At home, we don't use ammeters and voltmeters. We have an **electricity meter** to measure the amount of electrical energy we use.

Measuring energy in the lab

In the lab, you can use an energy meter to measure the amount of energy transferred by an electric current to a heater.

current

power supply | energy meter | heater

- The current flows from the power supply, through the meter to the heater.
- Then it must flow back through the meter to the supply, so that the meter can measure the change in energy.

The energy meter measures energy in **joules (J)**.

activity

Using an energy meter

Try these experiments with an energy meter.

- Connect the meter to a heater (see the photo). Put water in the heater and find out how much energy we need to heat the water by 10°C.
- Connect the meter to a lamp. How much energy does it use each minute? Try changing the voltage or using a different lamp.

⚠ Safety: Take care when using mains electricity.

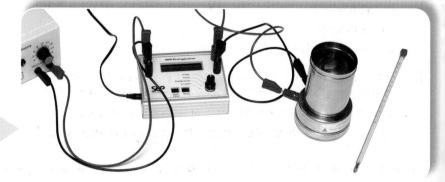

Using an energy meter to measure the energy supplied to a water heater

When the bill arrives ...

Most houses and flats have their own electricity meters. As you use electricity, the meter shows the amount of energy consumed.

The meter shows the amount of energy used in kilowatt-hours (kWh), often simply called 'units'. The meter in the photo shows that 11 483 units have been consumed since it was installed.

A domestic electricity meter – it measures the consumption of electrical energy from the mains supply

> **a** Where is the electricity meter in the house or flat where you live? When does the meter get read?

To calculate the cost of electricity, simply take the number of units consumed and multiply by the cost of each unit. The bill shows how the calculation is done.

ECOSPARK ELECTRIC

Ms V. Green
13A Fuse Close
Amperton

electricity bill: **£19.43**

Bill summary

Previous meter reading	27043
Latest meter reading	27289
Units consumed	246

246 units @ 13p per unit   £34.98

> **b** If you use 150 units of electricity and each unit costs 14 p, what will your bill be?

Big consumers

Some household appliances consume energy much faster than others.

- Appliances which produce a lot of heat use energy fast: heaters, tumble driers, etc.
- Appliances with large motors also use a lot of energy: washing machines, spin driers, etc.

Smaller appliances such as light bulbs, radios and electronic games use much less energy.

Great Debates

Modern flat-screen TVs use much more energy than the ones they have replaced. Should we go back to the old ones?

Summary Questions

1 What is the scientific unit of energy? Give its name and symbol.

2 What do each of these meters measure?
   a) ammeter
   b) voltmeter
   c) energy meter.

3 At the beginning of the week, a domestic electricity meter reads 11 404 units. At the end of the week, it reads 11 498 units.
   a) How many units have been used during the week?
   b) If each unit costs 14 p, what is the cost of the energy used?

KEY WORDS

electricity meter
joule (J)

Seeking Sustainability

- How can we use unsustainable energy sources responsibly?
- How can we make more use of sustainable energy sources?

Never again

Most of the electricity we use comes from power stations where coal or gas are burned. Some comes from nuclear power stations which use the energy stored in uranium.

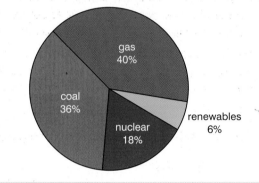

How we generate our electricity in the UK – figures for 2008

> **a** Study the pie chart. What percentage of our electricity is generated from fossil fuels?

Only a small fraction of our electricity comes from other sources such as wind power or hydroelectricity (water power).

Coal and gas are **fossil fuels**. When they are burned, they release carbon dioxide (CO_2) into the atmosphere. CO_2 is a greenhouse gas. It causes global warming which most scientists now believe is causing dangerous changes to the Earth's climate.

We can't go on like this – our use of fossil fuels is **unsustainable** in two ways:

- Our supplies will run out.
- We are harming our environment.

An alternative is **biofuel**, made from plants specially grown by farmers.

This coal-fired power station produces 2 million units every hour, but it's unsustainable. The rape seed growing in front can be used as a biofuel – that's sustainable

science@work

Scientists are trying to develop ways of burying the carbon dioxide produced by power stations. This process is called 'carbon sequestration'.

Sustainable thinking

Something is 'sustainable' if we can keep on doing it without producing problems in the future. Each generation should try to leave the world in a fit state for the next generation. It is unfair to expect people tomorrow to pay the price of our consumption today.

Wind power is an example of a sustainable energy source. The wind will always blow – it will never run out. People in centuries to come will be able to use wind turbines to generate electricity without using up a limited resource or damaging the atmosphere.

At the moment, most of our electricity is generated from unsustainable sources, so it makes sense to use them in a **responsible** way, for example by choosing energy-efficient appliances.

(b) Electricity can be generated using solar cells (photovoltaic cells). Is this sustainable or unsustainable?

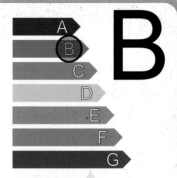

Modern appliances have a label to show how efficiently they use electricity

The nuclear question

- Some people think that nuclear power can be part of a sustainable energy supply. Nuclear power stations don't burn fossil fuels so they don't produce CO_2.

- However, other people disagree. They point out that nuclear power stations produce hazardous, radioactive waste which is very difficult to dispose of.

Stage a debate to decide between these two points of view.

Those on one side of the debate must explain why they think that nuclear power can be part of a sustainable electricity supply.

Those on the opposing side must explain why they disagree and how they would provide electricity sustainably in the future.

NUCLEAR POWER NO THANKS!   NUCLEAR POWER YES PLEASE!

Summary Questions

1 What fuels do we use to produce most of our electricity in the UK?

2 Fossil fuels are unsustainable but biofuels are sustainable. Explain why.

3 It isn't just electricity that relies on unsustainable sources of energy. Cars (and many other forms of transport) rely on fossil fuels.

   a) Is this sustainable? Explain your answer.

   b) How could we have a more sustainable transport system in the future? (You may have to do some research to find ideas for this.)

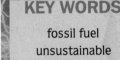

KEY WORDS

fossil fuel
unsustainable
biofuels
responsible

Around the Circuit

▶▶ How does current flow around a circuit?

▶▶ How is a voltage shared in a circuit?

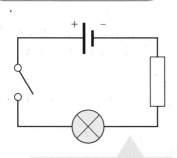

A series circuit – all of the components are connected end-to-end

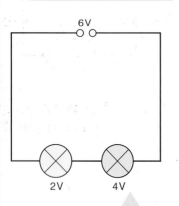

The voltage of the battery is shared between the two lamps

Did You know?

The volt is called after Alessandro Volta; the amp after André-Marie Ampère. They were two pioneers of electricity.

Series circuits

In a **series circuit**, the components are connected end-to-end so that they form a simple loop. The cell, battery or power supply provides the voltage needed to push current round the circuit.

> **a** Name the components shown in the circuit diagram.

Current flows from the positive terminal of the cell, through each component in turn. Then it flows back to the negative terminal of the cell. This means that:

> The current is the same at all points around a series circuit.

Don't forget that an electric current is a flow of electrons. These are particles, they can't just disappear or be used up.

Voltage in a series circuit

The next diagram shows what you may find if you measure the voltage across each component in a series circuit. In this circuit, the battery provides 6 V. There are two lamps. One has a voltage of 2 V across it; the other has 4 V across it. This shows that:

> In a series circuit, the voltage of the supply is shared between the components.

How can we understand this? The battery has to make the current flow through the two lamps, one after the other. Some of its voltage ('push') is used to push the current through the first lamp. The rest of its voltage is used to push the current through the second lamp.

activity

Try it with meters

Set up circuits as follows:

- Set up a series circuit and use one or more ammeters to show that the current has the same value all the way round.

- Set up a series circuit and use one or more voltmeters to show that the voltage of the supply is shared between the different components.

In each case, draw a circuit diagram and record your measurements on it.

The ammeter is measuring the current flowing through the resistor and the motor

Parallel circuits

In a **parallel circuit**, two or more components are connected side-by-side. In the circuit shown, each lamp 'feels' the full push of the cell. The voltage isn't shared between them.

Components in parallel have the same voltage across them.

b In the circuit shown, what is the voltage across each lamp?

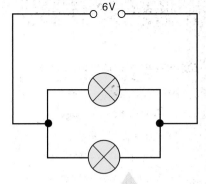

Current in a parallel circuit

If you connect two lamps in parallel, they both light up. This shows that they both have current flowing through them.

Picture the current flowing from the cell. It flows round from the positive terminal. When it reaches point X, it divides up – some flows through one lamp, some through the other. These two currents recombine when they reach point Y. Then they flow back to the cell.

Current is shared between components connected in parallel.

More with meters

Devise and explain a circuit to show that current is shared when components are connected in parallel. Draw a diagram to show your results.

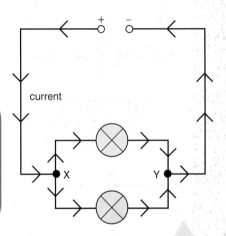

These two lamps are connected in parallel with each other

The current divides at X and joins up again at Y

Summary Questions

1 a) Which quantity is the same all the way round a series circuit?

b) Which quantity is shared between components connected in parallel?

2 a) Draw a circuit diagram in which two lamps are connected in series with a 6 V supply.

b) If a current of 2.5 A flows through one, what current flows through the other?

c) If the two lamps are identical, what will the voltage be across each of them?

3 Look at the second diagram on the opposite page.

a) Which lamp needs a bigger voltage to push the current through it?

b) What does this tell you about the resistances of the two lamps?

4 Copy the two circuit diagrams and mark on the missing values of current and voltage.

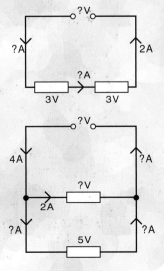

Energy and Voltage

How is energy transferred by electricity?

How can we picture energy changes in electric circuits?

DANGER OF DEATH
ELECTRICITY
KEEP OUT

RISK OF
ELECTRIC SHOCK

Did You Know?

New scientific discoveries are often used in ways that turn out to be dangerous.

Danger – high voltage!

Batteries are usually quite safe – their voltage will only make a very small current flow through you. The mains voltage is 230 V. This can easily make a fatal current flow through you.

An electric shock does two things:

- Because a current is flowing through you, it has a heating effect. It burns your skin and the liquid in your cells boils – nasty!
- At the same time, electricity can interfere with your nerves. Your muscles contract violently and your heart may stop beating.

> **a** Hazard signs are used to warn people about electrical dangers. Where have you seen such signs?

A patient is being given high voltage shocks – this therapy was tried to all sorts of illnesses, physical and mental

Even higher

When you see tall pylons with cables hanging between them, you can be sure that the voltage of the electricity is much higher than 230 V.

- In the UK, power stations generate electricity at 25 000 V.
- The **cables** which distribute electricity around the country work at voltages up to 400 000 V.

These high voltages mean that the current is carrying a great deal of energy.

Most people would prefer not to live as close as this to high voltage electricity cables if they could avoid it

Modelling current and energy

Electricity transfers energy from place to place. In a simple circuit like the one in the diagram:

- The current carries energy as it flows from the cell.
- It delivers the energy to the lamp which transforms it to light energy (and heat).
- The current returns to the cell having given up its energy.

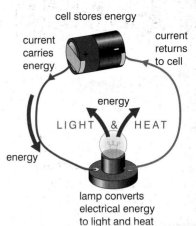

cell stores energy

current carries energy

current returns to cell

energy

LIGHT & HEAT

energy

energy

lamp converts electrical energy to light and heat

Make a model

In science, we often use **models** to help us picture ideas like this. Here is a model to explain circuits.

The picture shows a garden water feature. The pump sucks up water from the pool and squirts it out through the pipe. As the water flows down into the pool, it turns the little water wheel. Then it is ready to be sucked up again. In this model:

- The water flowing round represents the current.
- The pump represents the battery, giving potential energy to the water.
- The water wheel represents a lamp or other component which operates when the current flows.

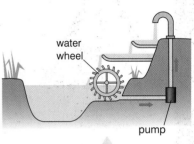

water wheel

pump

One way of modelling an electric circuit

activity

Understanding the model

With a partner, discuss the following:

- In the water model of an electric circuit, how can you tell that energy is being transferred to the water wheel?

- Where has the energy come from and how is it transferred to the wheel?

- How would you change the model to represent a circuit with a higher voltage battery in it?

Summary Questions

1 Put these voltages in order, from smallest to biggest:

      power station generator   **distribution cables**
        mains supply   **single cell**   **battery**

2 A cell is a store of chemical potential energy. When a current flows, some of this energy is converted to electrical energy.
Draw a diagram to represent this.

3 Draw a diagram to represent the energy changes that take place in an electric lamp.

4 A milkman drives from the dairy and delivers milk all round an estate. He returns to the dairy at the end of his round. How could this be a model for the way in which electricity transfers energy? Compare this with the water model above. Which is better? Why?

KEY WORDS

cable
model

know your stuff

▼ Question 1 (level 4)

Electricity is a good way of transferring energy from place to place. Imagine that you live on a remote island and that your electricity comes from a wind turbine, as shown in the picture.

The energy of the wind allows you to see TV programmes. Copy and complete the diagram to show the different forms of energy as it is transferred from place to place. (The first box has been completed for you.) [6]

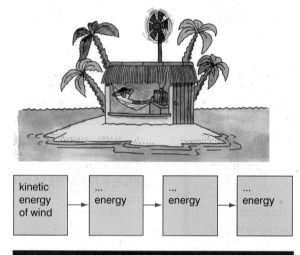

| kinetic energy of wind | → | ... energy | → | ... energy | → | ... energy |

▼ Question 2 (level 4)

You can't store electricity but there are other ways of storing energy. Copy and complete the table. For each example:

● Write how the energy is stored.

● Give an example of a way in which we could use the stored energy. [6]

Example of energy store	How energy is stored	One way to use the energy
A stretched rubber band		
A 9 V battery		
Water stored behind a dam		

▼ Question 3 (level 5)

Before he went camping, Mike charged up his rechargeable torch.

ⓐ What energy transfer took place as the batteries were recharged? Choose from:

chemical to electrical   light to electrical
electrical to light   electrical to chemical [1]

ⓑ What energy change took place when Mike used the torch in his tent at night? Choose from:

electrical to light
chemical to light   chemical to heat   [1]

▼ Question 4 (level 6)

Pip set up an electric circuit as shown. She included voltmeters to show the voltage across each lamp.

ⓐ Were the lamps connected in series or in parallel? [1]

ⓑ How many volts did the battery supply? [1]

Pip wanted to check the voltage of the battery. The picture shows the circuit diagram.

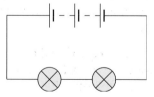

ⓒ Copy the diagram and add a voltmeter to show how Pip could measure the voltage of the battery. [1]

Pip also wanted to measure the current flowing around the circuit.

ⓓ On your diagram, mark with an A a point in the circuit where she could include an ammeter to do this. [1]

How Science Works

▼ Question 1 (level 5)

Max was investigating the heating effect of an electric current. He put an electric heater in a beaker of water and connected it to a power supply. He added a thermometer to measure the temperature of the water.

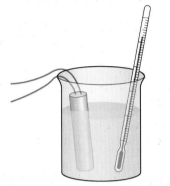

Max switched on the power supply and noted the temperature of the water every 5 minutes. The graph shows his results.

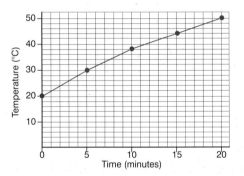

a What was the temperature of the water 15 minutes after the start of the experiment? [1]

b By how many degrees had the temperature of the water increased 15 minutes after the start of the experiment? [2]

c As the water got hotter, its temperature rose more and more slowly. How can you tell this from the graph? [1]

d Max thought his results might have been different if he had put some insulating material around the beaker before he switched on the heater. Suggest how this might have changed his results and explain your ideas. [3]

▼ Question 2 (level 6)

Nora was investigating a small wind turbine which was connected to an electrical generator. She used a fan to make the wind which turned the turbine. She connected the generator to a voltmeter to see what voltage it produced.

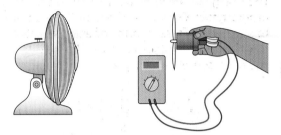

Nora placed the turbine 20 cm from the fan and switched the fan on. She waited to see the biggest reading on the voltmeter. Then she moved the turbine closer to the fan, 5 cm at a time. The table shows her results.

Distance from fan (cm)	Voltage from generator (V)
20	1.30
15	1.45
10	1.46
5	1.45

a What was the greatest value of voltage obtained by Nora? [1]

b Nora thought of several possible explanations for her results. For each of the following statements, say whether you think it might be supported by Nora's results. Explain your answer. [6]

  A The voltmeter may have been read incorrectly.

  B The wind gets stronger the closer you get to the fan.

  C The wind spreads out as it moves away from the fan.

Forces and Motion

Forces and motion

Flying, falling

In cartoons, the characters often move in strange ways. For example, someone is being chased. They run like mad; you can tell they are moving fast because they have speed streaks drawn behind them and the scenery rushes past in the opposite direction. Then they run off a cliff. They hang in mid-air, arms and legs thrashing. After a moment, they plummet straight downwards.

Everybody knows that real people or objects don't move like that, although it would be fun if they could. But how do real objects move? Scientists have put a lot of effort into finding out how to describe and predict the way things move.

a Look at the three photographs on this page. How can you describe the movement of the sprinter, the train and the parachutist?

Speed under control

The illustration of a man parachuting was published in 1595 by an Italian inventor, Fauste Veranzio. He constructed the parachute and tested it in Venice. It was fine for jumping off towers, but there were no aeroplanes to jump out of in those days.

Since about 1800, most parachutes have been made with a central hole in the canopy. This makes it easier to control them during the descent.

The Latin words 'homo volans' mean 'flying man'

A parachute is used to slow down the Space Shuttle as it comes in to land

Faster, slower

Take a sheet of paper and drop it. It will fall to the floor.

Throw a screwed-up sheet of paper through the air.
It follows a curved path.

Your task is to make a single sheet of paper fall as quickly as possible to the floor and then as slowly as possible.

- How can you design a fair test that will help you decide who in your class is the most successful at doing this?
- How can you record the path of a ball of paper as it flies through the air?

Measuring Speed

First in the race

When runners race against each other, the scoreboard usually shows their times. The person with the shortest time has run the fastest and wins the race.

RUNNER	TIME
8	12.5
21	12.8
40	13.9

The result of the 100 metres sprint

a Which runner in the picture was the fastest? Whose speed was the least?

Start and stop

When the car in the diagram is given a gentle push, it runs down the slope and along the table to the finishing line. How can you find out its speed?

Here's what you must do:

- Start the stopwatch when you let go of the car.
- Stop the stopwatch when it crosses the finishing line. This tells you the **time taken**.
- Use a metre rule to measure the **distance travelled** by the car.
- Now you can calculate the car's **average speed**:

$$\text{average speed} = \frac{\text{distance travelled}}{\text{time taken}}$$

Timing the car for the complete run will only tell you its *average* speed. This is because the car's speed changes. It speeds up as it runs down the slope. It slows down as it runs along the flat table.

b At which point is the car's speed greatest?

Sidebar:

▶▶ How can we measure the speed of a moving object?

▶▶ What do we mean by 'precision' when taking measurements?

Calculating speed

In July 2004, Philip Rabinowitz ran 100 m in 28.7 s. It was a world record – for a 100-year-old man! Unfortunately, the electronic timer broke down and his record didn't count.

Here is how to calculate his average speed:

$$\text{average speed} = \frac{100\,\text{m}}{28.7\,\text{s}} = 3.5\,\text{m/s}$$

The scientific unit of speed is metres per second (m/s).

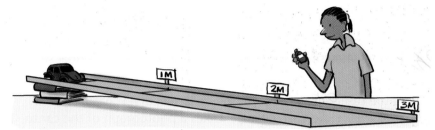

Thinking about precision

- In a marathon race, the winner might have a time of 2 hours 15 minutes and 20 seconds, shown as 2 h 15 m 20 s.
- When you use a stopwatch to time a toy car, the time taken might be 2.4 s.
- In a sprint race, the winner might have a time of 10.66 s.

The sprinter's time is measured with great **precision**. The runner-up might be just one-hundredth of a second (0.01 s) behind, so the electronic timer must measure to 0.01 s. That is not necessary in a marathon, the runners are usually farther apart.

c A stopwatch can only measure to 0.1 s. What fraction of a second is this?

... see a report of a new athletics record, notice how many decimal points are given.

activity

Speed check

- Make a car run down a long, gently sloping ramp. Use a stopwatch to find the time it takes to travel 1 m.
- (Make sure you repeat the measurement several times. Why is this important?)
- Repeat for 2 m and 3 m.
- Look at your results. Do you think this is a good way to find the car's speed? Can you suggest a better way?

Summary Questions

1. A snail crawls 10 cm in 2 minutes. A slug creeps 6 cm in 1 minute. Which slithers most quickly?

2. Work out the speed of each of the runners in the 100 m race (opposite).

3. The table shows the record breaking times for the women's 100 m sprint at the Olympic Games. What do you notice about the precision of these measurements? Why do you think this is important?

Date	Runner	Time (s)
1988	Florence Griffith Joyner	10.62
1984	Evelyn Ashford	10.97
1976	Annegret Richter	11.01
1964	Wyomia Tyus	11.2
1960	Wilma Rudolph	11.3
1952	Marjorie Jackson	11.5

4. Visit the website of the International Olympic Committee and find out how some other records have changed.

KEY WORDS

time taken
distance travelled
average speed
precision

Going Electronic

On the road

Some drivers don't like speed cameras – they slow down as they approach the camera, then speed up again when they are safely past. But how does a speed camera work? One type uses two electronic sensors buried in the road surface *before* the camera.

- As the front wheels of the car go over the first sensor, an electrical signal goes to the camera and its clock starts working.
- As the wheels go over the second sensor, a second signal stops the clock.

Now the camera can calculate the car's speed. If it has been travelling over the speed limit, it takes a photograph of the car to record its number plate.

> **a** The speed camera records the time taken by the car to travel from one sensor to the next. What else must it know to calculate the car's speed?

A 'Gatso' speed camera

Electronic speed measurement

There are problems with using a stopwatch to time a toy car. When you see the car pass the mark, it takes a little time for your brain to react and for your finger to press the button. This means that you don't get the same measurement each time. A better way to find the car's average speed is to use a **light gate**, connected to a computer. This will give you a more **accurate** answer. (Remember that an accurate measurement gives you the true value.)

Passing through a light gate

- When you release the car, it passes through the first light gate. The card on the car breaks the invisible beam and this starts the timer.
- When the car passes through the second light gate, it stops the timer.

Two gates – or one?

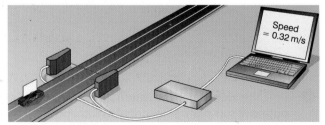

Speed = 0.32 m/s

One light gate is enough to measure a car's speed

How can you find the speed of a car in the lab? Here's how, using a single light gate:

- Fix a card to the top of the car. Pass the car through the light gate.
- The front edge of the card breaks the beam and starts the timer.
- When the back edge of the card passes out of the gate, the timer stops.

This tells you the time for the card to pass through the light gate.

b What else do you need to know, to find the car's speed?

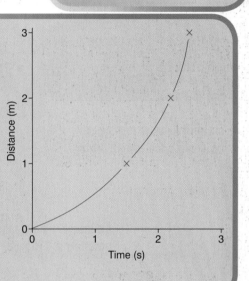

activity

Breaking the beam

- Set up a single light gate, connected to a computer.
- Use your light gate to measure a car's speed at different points down a slope.

activity

Speed check

Repeat the 'Speed check' experiment from P2.2 with the car running down the gently sloping ramp. Use two light gates to find its speed over 1 m, 2 m, and so on. If you're lucky, the computer will calculate the speed for you! (But you will have to input the distance between the two gates.)

- Repeat each measurement several times, to get an idea of how **reliable** your measurements are.
- How do your results compare with when you used a stopwatch?
- Use your results to draw a graph to show the distance travelled by the car in different times.

Summary Questions

1 A car takes 0.45 s to travel through the first light gate, and 0.54 s to travel through the next light gate. Is it speeding up or slowing down?

2 A toy car is 10 cm long. It takes 0.20 s to pass through a light gate. Calculate its speed.

3 Jensen used a stop clock to time a toy train as it travelled 2 m along the track. He repeated the measurement five times. Here are his results.

His teacher suggested that his answer might not be correct.

a) Look at Jensen's results. Give two reasons why it was a good idea to repeat the measurement five times.

b) What answer would you have deduced from Jensen's results? Explain your ideas.

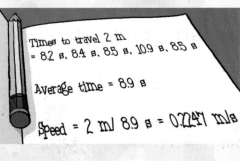

Times to travel 2 m
= 8.2 s, 8.4 s, 8.5 s, 10.9 s, 8.5 s

Average time = 8.9 s

Speed = 2 m/ 8.9 s = 0.2247 m/s

KEY WORDS

light gate
accurate
reliable

Going Steady

> ▸▸ How can we use graphs to represent motion?

You need to check your speed frequently when you are driving

Along the road

Driving instructors teach their students to drive at a steady speed. That's safer than speeding up and slowing down all the time. It means that other drivers will be able to judge what you will do next.

If you travel along a motorway at a steady speed of 110 km/h (kilometres per hour), after 1 hour you will have travelled 110 km. After 2 hours you will have travelled 220 km, and so on.

We can draw a **distance–time graph** to show a journey like this.

- The graph has time on the horizontal axis, and distance on the vertical axis.
- The graph is a straight line, because the car is travelling at a steady speed.

A distance–time graph for a car travelling at 110 km/h

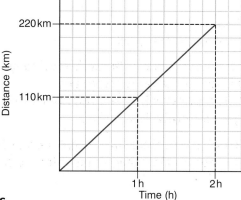

Different speeds

A distance–time graph can show the story of a journey. Look at this graph:

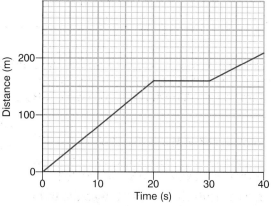

- At first the car is going at a steady speed; the graph slopes upwards.
- Then the car stops for a short time; the graph is horizontal (flat).
- Then the car moves off again, at a steady speed; the graph slopes upwards again.

ⓐ What are the units of time and distance on this graph?

Interpreting the graph

We can tell quite a lot of things from the distance–time graph like the one on the right. Here are two examples:

After 10 s, the car had travelled 80 m. We can calculate its speed:

$$\text{Speed} = \frac{\text{distance}}{\text{time}} = \frac{80\,m}{10\,s} = 8\,m/s$$

The car was stationary between 20 s and 30 s. We can calculate the time for which it was stationary:

$$\text{Time} = 30\,s - 20\,s = 10\,s$$

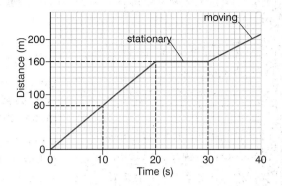

b How far had the car travelled when it came to a halt?

Graph slopes

Look at the **slope of the graph**.

- At first it is quite steep – the car is moving quite fast.
- Then it is level – the car is stationary.
- Then it slopes upwards again, but not as steeply. The car is moving more slowly than before.

So the slope of the distance–time graph tells us how fast the car is moving. The steeper the slope, the greater the speed.

activity

Graphic stories

- Draw a distance–time graph to represent a journey. It might be a trip to the shops, or how you walk to school.
- Show your graph to a partner. Ask them to describe your journey in words.
- Then swap over and describe your partner's journey.

Summary Questions

1 Two cars, red and blue, were waiting at the traffic lights. When the lights changed, they set off. The graph shows how they moved. Which car moved faster? How can you tell?

2 The graph shows the journey of a train.

a) Between which two points was the train stationary? Explain how you can tell.

b) Between which two points was the train moving fastest? Explain how you can tell.

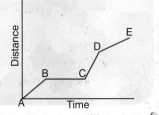

KEY WORDS

distance–time graph
slope of the graph

Changing Speed, Changing Direction

On your marks

Sprinters use starting blocks to get off to a flying start. The gun goes off, they push backwards on to the blocks and suddenly they are moving rapidly forwards. It takes a big forward **force** to get them moving.

On your marks... ready to accelerate forwards

A car driver knows how to change speed. Pushing down on the accelerator provides the force needed to make the car go faster. The force pushes forwards on the car, making it **accelerate** (speed up).

If the driver wants to slow down, he or she pushes on the brake pedal. The brakes provide a force in the opposite direction to the force of the engine, slowing the car down.

On the ice

Ice skaters can move even faster than sprinters. How do they do it? Ice skating is easy – once you've got moving. There is almost no friction to slow you down, so you go along at almost constant speed in a straight line. To change direction, you have to push sideways on the ice. (Roller blading is similar.)

Smooth movers – there is little friction to slow these skaters

a How would you slow down if you were an ice skater?

> ▶▶ How can we make an object speed up or slow down?
>
> ▶▶ What happens when the forces on an object are balanced?

activity

Forces and sports

Think about how forces are important in sports. Find photographs – look on the sports' pages of newspapers and magazines, and on the internet – showing sports in action. Find examples where:

- Someone, or something, is moving at a steady speed, because there is no force to slow it down.
- Someone, or something (e.g. a ball), is speeding up or slowing down, because of a force.
- Someone, or something, is changing direction, because of a force.

Prepare a presentation. For each example, name the force that is causing the movement to change (e.g. the force of the racket on the ball). Be prepared to show your best examples to the rest of the class.

This athlete provides a strong force to start the ball flying through the air

Balanced and unbalanced forces

If you are setting off on a bicycle, you have to turn the pedals quite hard. Then there is a force which starts you moving. The diagram shows how to represent the force with a labelled arrow.

Forward force

Braking force

Thrust

Weight

To slow down, you apply the brakes. Now there is a backwards force, slowing you down.

Often, there are several forces at work. The rocket in the diagram will go faster and faster as it takes off, because the forces on it are **unbalanced**. The thrust is greater than its weight.

b What would happen to the rocket if the upward thrust was less than its weight? Draw a diagram to show this situation.

So here is what can happen to an object if the forces on it are unbalanced:

- It can accelerate (go faster) – this includes starting to move.
- It can slow down.
- It can change direction (this needs a sideways force).

If the forces on an object are **balanced**:

- It will move at a steady speed in a straight line.
- Or it will stay at rest.

c Look at the photo of the spacecraft in space. Why is there no friction to slow it down?

There are no forces on a spacecraft when it is far out in space, so it will move steadily ahead. It doesn't need to fire its rockets to keep going

Summary Questions

1 An unbalanced force is needed to make an object:

  A speed up   B slow down

  C change direction   D all of these.

2 Use the idea of forces to explain why it would be very difficult for a runner to sprint on an ice rink.

3 There are four forces acting on a powerboat: its weight, the upthrust of the water, drag and the forward thrust of its motor. Draw a diagram to show these forces. If the boat is going at a steady speed in a straight line, which pairs of forces must be balanced? How could the rider change direction?

KEY WORDS

force
accelerate
unbalanced forces
balanced forces

It's a Drag

- How does air resistance affect moving objects?
- How can we reduce the effects of drag on moving objects?
- How can I plan a fair test to investigate drag?

Racing cyclists try to avoid air resistance

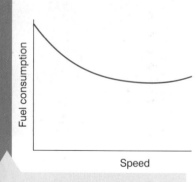

Fuel consumption / Speed

Cars use more fuel when moving very slowly or very quickly

Moving through fluids

It is said that racing cyclists often shave their legs so that they will travel faster. Hairy legs mean more **air resistance**, which slows you down. Today's top cyclists usually wear body hugging Lycra outfits to help them slip through the air with less resistance.

a Does air resistance increase or decrease as you move faster? How do you know?

Efficient driving

Motorists should be concerned about the efficiency of their cars. They want to travel as many kilometres as possible for each litre of fuel they use. Manufacturers must advertise information about the fuel consumption of their cars. The government also publishes data for all makes of car.

The graph shows how much fuel a typical car uses at different speeds.

- At high speeds, it uses a lot of fuel for each kilometre travelled, because air resistance is greater.
- At low speeds, it uses a lot of fuel, because car engines don't work very efficiently at low speeds.

You can see that the car uses less fuel at 'in-between' speeds, when the engine is working well and there isn't too much air resistance.

Better design

We design cars with a **streamlined** shape to reduce the effects of air resistance. You may have seen lorries with wind deflectors on top of the cab. These help to push air up over the top of the lorry so that it uses less fuel.

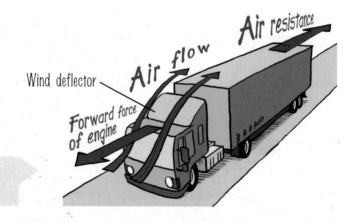

This lorry is shaped to reduce air resistance

b Give an example of a streamlined animal and explain why streamlining is important for it.

As a car or lorry travels along the road, it has to push air out of the way. A lorry travelling at 70 mph (31 m/s) pushes aside as much as 1 tonne of air every second. Pushing that much air around takes a lot of energy. That's why cars and lorries use more fuel at top speed, and fuel costs money.

The resistance of water

People with damaged limbs may be encouraged to take exercise in water, to help build up their muscles. They have to struggle against the resistance of water, which is known as **drag**.

If you try to move through water, you will experience more resistance than when moving through air. Water is much denser than air. Therefore you have to push many more kilograms of mass out of the way when you move through water than when you move through air.

Controlling drag

- Fill a tall glass or clear plastic container with water. Drop a small ball of Plasticine into the water and watch it sink to the bottom.
- How can you control the rate at which the Plasticine falls? Can you make it go faster or slower?
- Think up your own scientific question and investigate it.

Did You Know?

The fastest self-powered animal is the peregrine falcon with reliably verified dive speeds of up to 200 km/h. They can fly horizontally at over 50 km/h too.

To swim, you have to push your way through the water

Next time you...

... go swimming, try walking through the water. The deeper the water, the harder it is as the drag increases.

Summary Questions

1. Name the forces that tend to slow things down as they move through air, and through water.

2. Explain why a racehorse can increase its strength more effectively by swimming rather than by galloping around.

3. A century ago, cars didn't travel very fast. How can you tell this from the shape of the car in the photo?

4. The resistance of water slows you down when you are swimming. However, you wouldn't be able to swim at all without drag. Explain why not. (Hint: think about why it is impossible to swim through air.)

KEY WORDS

air resistance
streamlined
drag

Going Up, Coming Down

> ▶▶ What causes objects to fall?
>
> ▶▶ How does a falling object move?
>
> ▶▶ How can I plan a fair test to investigate air resistance?

Up in a balloon

If you want to go up in a balloon, you will have to understand about forces. The balloon rises up because it is filled with hot air which is less dense than the cooler air surrounding it. This means that the **upthrust** is greater than the **weight** of the balloon.

Going up...

When the balloon reaches the right height, the forces on it must be balanced. Let some of the hot air out of the balloon, so that the upthrust and weight are equal.

Forces on a hot air balloon

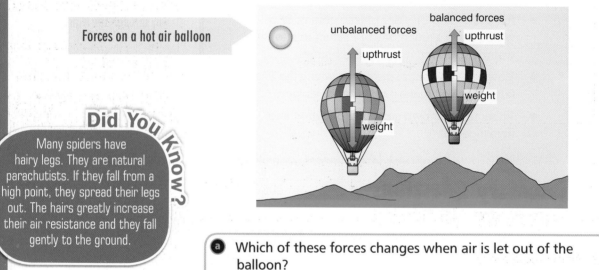

a Which of these forces changes when air is let out of the balloon?

> ### Did You Know?
> Many spiders have hairy legs. They are natural parachutists. If they fall from a high point, they spread their legs out. The hairs greatly increase their air resistance and they fall gently to the ground.

Parachuting down

Now is the time to jump out of your balloon, but don't forget your parachute! At first, you go faster and faster as you accelerate towards the ground. Then you pull the cord and your parachute opens. A big force slows you down to a safe speed for landing.

What is that big force? It's **air resistance**, of course. The parachute has a big area and you are moving very fast. Both of these **factors** mean that there's a lot of air resistance, which is vital if you aren't going to hit the ground at high speed.

The graph shows your journey down to the ground.

Distance–time graph for a parachutist

b At which point on the graph are you travelling fastest?

The big drop

Free-fall parachutists don't open their parachutes until they are quite close to the ground. At first, they fall faster and faster, until they reach their top speed. When they open their parachutes, they slow down to a safe speed.

The graph shows how a parachutist's speed changes as they fall. A **speed–time graph** like this tells a story. You can interpret the graph using your knowledge of forces and how they affect the way things move.

Speed

Speed–time graph for a parachutist

parachute opens

getting faster

slowing down

safe speed

landing

Time

Athletes use parachutes to provide resistance during their training sessions

Summary Questions

① Name these forces:
   a) pulls downwards on all objects on the Earth
   b) pushes upwards on a floating object.

② Imagine that you are up in a balloon, floating at a steady height. How could you change the forces acting on your balloon to make it go:
   a) higher?
   b) down to the ground?

   Draw force diagrams to illustrate your answers.

③ Look at the graph above, showing the free-fall parachutist's drop.
   a) How can you tell from the graph that the parachutist goes faster and faster at the start of the drop?
   b) How can you tell from the graph that the parachutist falls more slowly after the parachute opens?
   c) At which of the points marked on the graph are the forces on the parachutist balanced?

KEY WORDS

upthrust
weight
air resistance
factor
speed–time graph

High Pressure, Low Pressure

- ▸▸ What does the word 'pressure' mean in science?
- ▸▸ How can we calculate pressure?

The pressure builds up

The word 'pressure' has a special meaning in science. Here's one way to understand it:

Imagine that your friend has been playing on a frozen pond. Suddenly the ice breaks and he falls through. You are on the bank – how can you save him?

You notice a ladder lying nearby. You lay the ladder across the ice, crawl to your friend and pull him onto the ladder. You are both safe.

Thin ice is likely to break if you stand on it. Your weight is too great when you are standing upright. However, if you spread your weight out over a bigger area, you should be safe.

> **a** Is your weight less when you use the ladder?

We say that the **pressure** is less when your weight is spread over a bigger area. A small **force** on a big **area** gives a small pressure. A big force on a small area gives a high pressure.

> **b** When you stand upright on the ice, what is the 'small area' your weight is pushing on? Why would it be more dangerous to stand on one foot rather than two?

Pressure at work

By thinking about pressure, you can understand things from both the natural world and the technological world. For example:

A camel has big feet, with splayed-out toes. This is useful if it is walking on soft desert sand. Its weight is spread over a large area. This means that the pressure on the sand is less and the camel is less likely to sink in.

At some time in your life, you must have had an injection. Doctors use needles which are very thin and pointed. This means that the force pressing on your skin is concentrated on a tiny area. The pressure is high and the needle pushes easily through your skin.

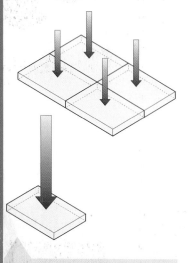

The same force spread over a bigger area gives lower pressure

Calculating pressure

The pressure caused by a force depends on two quantities:

- The size of the force (in N).
- The area it is pressing on (in cm² or m²).

Here's the equation to work out pressure:

$$\text{pressure} = \frac{\text{force}}{\text{area}}$$

Now here's how to work out the pressure of a person weighing 800 N standing on the floor; the soles of their shoes have an area of 20 cm²:

$$\text{pressure} = \frac{\text{force}}{\text{area}} = \frac{800\,\text{N}}{20\,\text{cm}^2} = 40\,\text{N/cm}^2$$

c An easy question: What is the pressure of a 500 N force pressing on an area of 1 cm²?

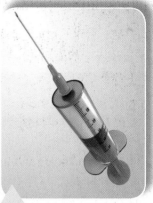

A sharply pointed needle looks alarming, but it requires a smaller force to puncture your skin than a fatter needle

force

area

Investigating pressure

activity

Piling on the pressure

You can compress plastic foam by placing weights on it.

- Find a block of foam. Place a wooden board on top and add weights. Calculate the pressure.

- Find out how the thickness of the foam changes as the pressure increases. How does the thickness change as the pressure increases?

⚠ **Safety:** Protect feet, hands and the bench from falling weights.

Summary Questions

1. Copy the following sentence *twice*, choosing one word from each pair, to give two different sentences about pressure:

   A **big/small** force pressing on a **big/small** area gives a **high/low** pressure.

2. Calculate the pressure when a force of 100 N presses on an area of 5 m².

3. Draw up a table like the one shown. Fill the four boxes with examples from the natural and technological worlds.

   Here are some examples. Add some more of your own.

   snow shoes   pins and needles   ducks' feet   bee stings
   skis   ice skates   sharks' teeth

Natural world: force concentrated on small area	Technological world: force concentrated on small area
Natural world: force spread over large area	Technological world: force spread over large area

Pressure in Liquids and Gases

- ▶▶ How can we show that liquids and gases exert pressure?
- ▶▶ Why do liquids and gases exert pressure?

Blowing up and lying down

Blow up a balloon. You have to press hard on the air to push it into the balloon. When the balloon is blown up, you know that the air inside is under pressure – just pop it with a pin.

a Why is it easier for your heart to pump blood to your head if you are lying down?

Blowing hard – it looks like he might burst a blood vessel!

The air inside a balloon presses outwards in all directions so that the balloon is almost spherical. In the same way, the blood in your body pushes outwards in all directions. If you cut a major artery, the result can be both dramatic and dangerous. Try not to spring a leak!

The air inside a balloon presses outwards, keeping it inflated

Going down

Submarines are designed to dive deep in the sea. Some research submarines carry divers hundreds of metres below the surface. It's very dark down there and the pressure of the water is huge.

The further down the submarine goes, the greater the pressure. Why is this? The answer is simple. The weight of the water above the submarine presses down on it – that's the force that creates the pressure on the submarine.

To withstand the pressure, the submarine is made of thick sheets of steel. The windows are of thick, strong plastic. It's best if the submarine has a spherical or cylindrical shape.

The submarine must withstand the pressure of the water above it

Did You Know?

Many of the molecules which make up the air around you are moving at over 400 m/s – that's fast!

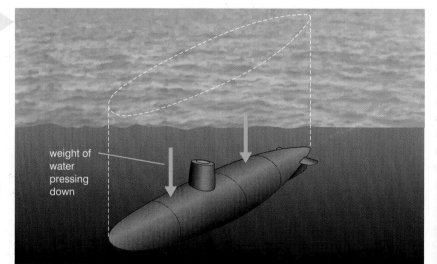

weight of water pressing down

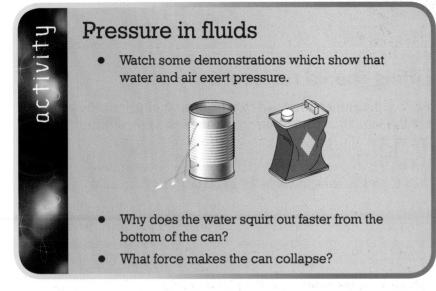

activity

Pressure in fluids

- Watch some demonstrations which show that water and air exert pressure.

- Why does the water squirt out faster from the bottom of the can?
- What force makes the can collapse?

Particles and pressure

Liquids and gases (such as water and air) are **fluids** – they are substances that can flow. They press outwards in all directions. Why do fluids exert pressure? We can use the **particle model** to answer this question.

Liquids and gases are made of particles which can move about. Think about the particles of air in a balloon. As they move, they bump into the inside surface of the balloon. Each little bump gives a little push. There are billions and trillions of pushes each second on every square centimetre. All these add up to the pressure of the air on the balloon.

In the same way, the air presses on you. You don't feel the individual particles as they collide with you, but the total effect is large.

b Why don't you feel the particles of the air pressing on your skin?

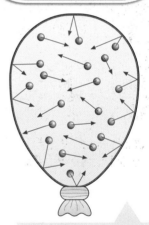

The air particles in a balloon create the pressure needed to keep it inflated

Summary Questions

1. Explain why there is a large pressure on the bottom of a swimming pool. Where is the pressure greatest in a pool?

2. Use the idea of particles to explain why the air presses with a strong force on a glass window pane. Why doesn't the window get pushed in by the pressure of the air outside?

3. a) The higher you go in the atmosphere, the less dense it is. Use the particle model to explain why this makes the pressure less.

   b) If you climb a mountain or go up in an aircraft, your ears may pop. Find out why the lower pressure makes this happen.

KEY WORDS

fluid
particle model

Levers Everywhere

▶▶ What is a lever?

▶▶ What can levers do for us?

Lifting the lid on levers

What is the easiest way to lift the lid of a tin of paint? The lid fits tightly (so that air cannot get in), so it can be very difficult to get the lid off.

Use a screwdriver. Put the end of the screwdriver under the edge of the lid, and lever it upwards. Hey presto! It's off.

You are using the screwdriver as a **lever**. People have used levers for thousands of years. For example, the ancient Egyptians used levers to help in lifting some of the stones for the pyramids. A lever allows you to move something which, unaided, would require a bigger force.

a A cyclist may have a set of tyre levers. What job is easier using tyre levers?

Finding the pivot

How does the 'screwdriver–paint tin lid' lever work? The diagram shows two forces:

- The force you exert, pushing down on the handle of the screwdriver. This force is called the **effort**.
- The force exerted by the lid on the tip of the screwdriver, which the screwdriver has to overcome. This force is called the **load**.

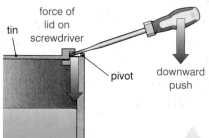

Opening a tin of paint

This wouldn't work if there wasn't something else: the rim of the paint tin. The lever touches the rim, and this point is the **pivot** of the lever. As you push down on one end, the other end moves up. The pivot is the point which doesn't move.

A wheelbarrow acts like a lever. You lift the handles, and the heavy load in the barrow is raised off the ground.

b Where is the pivot of a pair of scissors? Where is the pivot of a wheelbarrow-lever?

Forces on a wheelbarrow

lifting force

weight

activity

A look at levers

Examine some examples of levers. In each case, look for three things:

- the pivot
- the effort (the force that you apply to the lever)
- the load (the force that you are trying to overcome by using the lever).

Link up to...
TECHNOLOGY
You have probably made devices in technology that make use of levers. Many toys, for example, have levers in them.

Lifting a load

Why do we use levers? They allow us to do things which we might be too weak to do without a lever. For example, you would find it hard to lift a paving slab, but it's much easier if you use a lever. The picture shows how this works. You can see two things:

- Your effort force pushing downwards is smaller than the load you are trying to lift upwards.
- Your effort is further from the pivot; the load is closer to the pivot.

That's why levers are so useful. They can allow us to use a smaller force to move a bigger load. But this only works if our force is further from the pivot.

weight   lifting force

Lifting a paving slab

> **c** Think about a wheelbarrow. Which is closer to the pivot, your lifting force or the weight of the load in the barrow? Which requires less force, lifting the load by hand, or lifting it in the wheelbarrow?

Turning effect

A force makes a lever turn about the pivot. We say it has a **turning effect**. The bigger the force and the further away it is from the pivot, the greater its turning effect.

By moving a force so that it is twice as far from the pivot, you can double its turning effect.

Next time you...
... lift a heavy object, think about the levers in your body that make this possible. There are dozens of bony levers in our skeletons – even the three little bones in the inner ear act as levers to make the vibrations of sound bigger.

Summary Questions

1. What name is given to the point about which a lever turns?

2. An ancient (or modern) Egyptian could use a lever to lift a large block of stone:
   a) Draw a diagram to show this. What would they use for the pivot?
   b) Add force arrows to your diagram. Label the load and the effort.
   c) Which force is greater, the weight of the block or the push of the Egyptian?
   d) How could you increase the turning effect of the effort?

3. Imagine that you had to lift a heavy brick in a wheelbarrow. Where in the barrow should you put the brick, to make it easiest to lift?

KEY WORDS
lever
effort
load
pivot
turning effect

Getting Balanced

▸▸ How can we calculate the turning effect of a force?

▸▸ When is a lever balanced?

See-saw sums

A see-saw is a type of lever. A single adult can balance two small children. Alternatively, one small child can balance a large one. The small child must sit further from the pivot to increase the turning effect of their weight.

Another name for the turning effect of a force is its **moment**. The moment of a force is the size of the force multiplied by its distance from the pivot:

moment = force × distance from pivot

(The word 'moment' here means 'effect'; it's a bit like 'a momentous event', which is an event that has a big effect.)

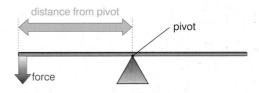

Calculating moments

If a force of 20 N presses down at a distance of 3 m from a pivot, its moment is:

moment = 20 N × 3 m = 60 Nm

The unit of moment is the newton-metre (Nm), because we are multiplying newtons by metres.

> ⓐ Find the moment of a 10 N force acting 4 m from a pivot.

You can use this idea to see if a see-saw is **balanced**. In the picture:

● The 30 N force is pressing down to the right of the pivot; it is trying to turn the see-saw clockwise.
● The 20 N force is pressing down to the left of the pivot; it is trying to turn the see-saw anticlockwise.

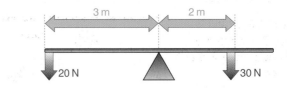

To work out if the see-saw is balanced, we calculate the moment of each force:

moment of 30 N force: 30 N × 2 m = 60 Nm

moment of 20 N force: 20 N × 3 m = 60 Nm

So the two forces have equal moments. They are trying to turn the see-saw in opposite directions, so their effects cancel each other out. The see-saw is balanced.

> **ⓑ** Which has a greater moment: a force of 10 N acting at 2 m from the pivot, or a force of 20 N acting at 1 m?

In the balance

If the turning effects of the forces on a lever cancel out, then the lever is balanced. In other words, the clockwise moments must equal the anticlockwise moments. We call this the **principle of moments**.

activity

Testing the principle of moments

Set up a ruler on a pivot. Place a weight on either side, so that it balances. If you make suitable measurements, you can work out the moment of each force. They should be equal.

Your task is to devise a **systematic** way of showing that the principle of moments is correct.

Method 1: Move one of the weights in even steps, and find the balancing position of the other weight.

Method 2: Change one of the weights, and find the weight that will balance it.

For each method, draw up a table which will allow you to show whether your results support the principle of moments.

Now extend your enquiry: Have a single weight on one side of the pivot and two weights at different positions on the other. How can you work out the moment of two weights?

Summary Questions

❶ Look at the diagram. Force *F* is pushing down on a beam.

a) Is force *F* trying to turn the beam clockwise or anticlockwise?

b) Which arrow shows the correct distance used for calculating the moment of force *F*?

❷ A force of 50 N pushes on a lever, 0.4 m from the pivot. What is the moment of the force?

❸ Look at the diagram. The see-saw is balanced. What is the size of the force *X*?

KEY WORDS

moment
balanced
principle of moments
systematic

know your stuff

▼ Question 1 (level 4)

Three children were playing on a see-saw. The table shows their weights.

Anne	600 N
Ben	650 N
Cath	570 N

a Anne sat on one end of the see-saw. There was no one on the other end. In which direction did Anne's end move? [1]

b Then Ben sat on the opposite end. He sat at the same distance from the pivot as Anne. How would the see-saw move? Explain your answer. [2]

c Cath took Ben's place on the see-saw. She wanted the see-saw to be balanced. Who should sit closer to the pivot, Anne or Cath? Explain your answer. [2]

▼ Question 2 (level 6)

The force diagrams show a car going at different speeds. The table gives four descriptions of the car's motion.

Decide which diagram matches each description. Copy the table and complete it to show which diagram matches each description, together with a reason for your choice. [8]

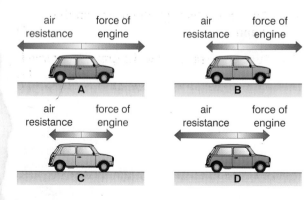

Description	Diagram	Reason
The car is speeding up.		
The car is slowing down.		
The car is travelling slowly at a steady speed.		
The car is travelling quickly at a steady speed.		

▼ Question 3 (level 7)

The graph shows how Sally won the 100 m sprint race.

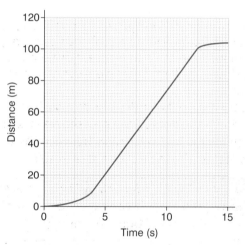

a Copy the graph. On your copy:

  (i) Mark with an A one point when Sally was running her fastest. [1]

  (ii) Mark with a B the point when Sally crossed the finishing line. [1]

b (i) For most of the race, Sally ran at a steady speed. How can you tell this from the graph? [1]

  (ii) During this time, were the forces on her balanced or unbalanced? [1]

c After how many seconds did Sally cross the finishing line? [1]

d Work out Sally's average speed in the race. [2]

How Science Works

▼ Question 1 (level 4)

Ali and Joe were studying the movement of a trolley as it ran down a gentle slope.

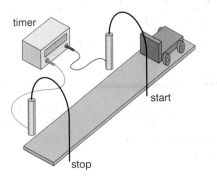

They positioned two light gates on the slope. One was fixed near the top of the slope. They positioned the other at different distances down the slope. The light gates were connected to a timer.

The boys gave the trolley a gentle push so that it ran down the slope. The timer showed the time taken for the trolley to move between the two light gates. The table shows their results.

Distance between light gates (m)	First attempt: time (s)	Second attempt: time (s)	Third attempt: time (s)	Average time (s)
1.20	0.37	0.48	0.35	0.40
2.00	0.60	0.66	0.78	

 a Calculate the average time for the trolley to travel 2.00 m. [2]

b Calculate the average speed of the trolley when it travelled 1.20 m. Give the correct unit. [2]

The boys were not very happy with their results. They seemed to vary a lot. Joe suggested that it would have been better if they had just made a single measurement.

c Explain why Joe was wrong. [2]

d What weakness in the design of their experiment could have led to their repeat readings being so varied? [1]

▼ Question 2 (level 6)

Emma was investigating the effect of pressure on plastic foam. She placed different weights on a block of foam and measured its thickness each time.

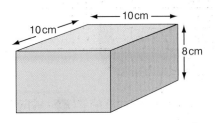

The picture shows the block of foam.

a What is the area of the top surface of the block? [1]

b What was the pressure on the block when Emma placed a 20 N weight on it? [2]

The table shows Emma's results:

Weight (N)	Thickness of block (cm)	Change in thickness (cm)
20	7.0	1.0
50	5.5	2.5
100	4.5	
150	4.0	

c Explain how Emma calculated the change in thickness of the block. [1]

d Calculate the values for the two empty spaces in the table. [2]

e Plot a graph to show Emma's results. [2]

f Draw a line through the points on the graph. [1]

g Suggest a reason why the graph is a curved line. [1]

How Science Works

- ▸▸ What are genetically modified crops?
- ▸ What are the advantages and disadvantages of growing genetically modified crops?

Media messages

You might have heard of GM crops or GM foods. GM stands for **genetically modified**. Scientists have used genetic engineering to change the genes in plants. This affects some characteristic of the plant so that the plant produces a better harvest.

GM foods are made from GM crops. Many people are worried about the consequences of growing GM crops. Some of the media have even called them Frankenstein food!

a Why do you think some people call GM food Frankenstein food?

GM soya beans

- Soya beans are an important source of protein in many parts of the world.
- Soya beans have been **genetically modified** to make them resistant to weed killer.
- Farmers plant **GM soya**. When the field contains lots of weeds the farmer sprays it with weed killer. The weeds get killed but the soya does not. *Brilliant!*

> These GM soya beans save me a lot of work. I used to have to employ people to weed the fields every day. Now I just spray them with weed killer. Mind you, the seeds are more expensive than the ones I used to use and I have to buy them every year. I'm not allowed to save them.

> These seeds are patented. That is excellent for my company because the farmers have to buy seeds every year. They are also good for local people because they increase crop yield.

> These seeds are really bad for the environment as farmers are encouraged to spray a lot of weed killer. Some weed killer drifts into the rainforest and kills more plants there.

I used to work as a farm labourer, weeding the farmer's fields but he doesn't need me now so I don't have a job any more.

I don't grow GM soya. I usually weed my fields by hand but I sometimes use weed killer as well. I am worried that the GM soya might cross with wild plants and make them resistant to weed killer as well.

This GM soya is cheaper than the other type. That leaves me more money to spend on other things so I am in favour of it.

GM soya

Write a newspaper article about GM soya. Make it **balanced** – point out the advantages and disadvantages to farmers and how they affect the environment.

There are many other examples of genetically modified food crops:

Self protecting plants – genetically engineered to produce a chemical, normally found in bacteria, that kills insects feeding on the crop.

Drought-resistant plants – that can grow better in dry soils.

Disease-resistant plants – that are not affected by microbes.

Easily digested plants – that are more nutritious so that animals and people do not need to eat so much.

Summary Questions

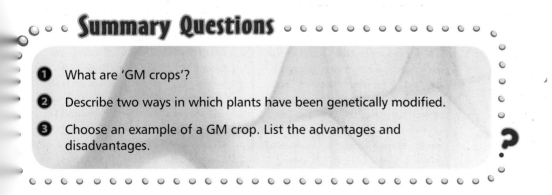

1. What are 'GM crops'?

2. Describe two ways in which plants have been genetically modified.

3. Choose an example of a GM crop. List the advantages and disadvantages.

How Science Works

▸▸ Why is it so important to conserve the Amazon rainforest?

▸▸ How does gold mining affect the forest?

▸▸ What are the issues to consider for the future of gold mining in Brazil?

Trouble in the rainforest

Brazil is one of the world's largest producers of gold. It is the largest country in South America. However, people are worried about the effects of gold mining on one of our planet's greatest natural resources – the Amazon rainforest. Some call it 'the lungs of the Earth'.

ⓐ Why do people call the Amazon rainforest 'the lungs of the Earth'? (*Hint:* Think about photosynthesis.)

Two-thirds of the 2.7 million square mile Amazon basin lies within Brazil. There is a debate raging about the rights and wrongs of gold mining.

Here are the views of some of the people involved:

The Amazon rainforest is being slowly poisoned by mercury released by private gold miners – the garimpeiros. The Amazon belongs to the people of the world and future generations. It contains over half the world's plant and animal species and one-third of the trees on Earth. We must protect it!

I am a garimpeiro. I have a wife and eight children in the shanty town outside the city of Rio de Janeiro. There is no way I'll ever get work there. The Amazon rainforest offers us our only chance to escape poverty. I can earn a decent wage mining gold.

We have passed laws to reduce the threat of mercury poisoning in the environment. The problem is that the garimpeiros use mercury in their sieves to extract gold from the rock they mine or silt they dredge from rivers. The mercury escapes into the air and a lot is also washed into the rivers with the waste rock.

We have tried to force the garimpeiros to use new equipment called a closed retort. But they won't obey the law! We banned the sale of mercury, but then they just bought it from unlicensed dealers. How can we stop them when we have so few police and such a massive area to patrol – it's impossible.

We have created reservations for the native Indian tribes to live in. In effect we have donated 10% of Brazil's land to 0.3% of our population. This has not been a popular decision with many people in Brazil. The garimpeiros are trespassing on land we have given to the native Indian tribes. Anyway, we now find that some Indians have sold miners the rights to use their land.

And now the rich countries of the West are telling us that we should stop exploiting the Amazon rainforest. That is easy for them to say, but that is where our country's wealth – its natural resources – lies. If we are to become wealthy we must be allowed to do what we feel is right for the people of Brazil.

activity

The great gold debate

There is going to be a debate on Brazilian TV about gold mining.

- Choose one person to be the host of the programme.
- Then pick a role to play from the interested parties you think should be invited to talk.
- Hold the debate.

My tribe has hunted in this forest since time began. Now we find men with guns on our land. They dump dirt into our rivers and there are less fish now. We have been told not to eat the fish anyway because they could make us very ill. But we have no choice; it's eat fish or go hungry.

We are finding more and more people coming to our hospital with symptoms of mercury poisoning. It attacks the central nervous system. But what is really worrying is that we are finding cases 200 miles from the gold mining activity. This is because the mercury is absorbed by the fish which people eat.

My children are destitute since I lost my husband gold mining. He sent us good money for a couple of months and we were planning to move to a proper house. But then came the news that he had died from a serious infection of the lungs caused by inhaling mercury vapour. Now I just don't know what to do.

Don't think that it's just jewellers that use gold. Here are some of the other users of gold:
- Computer, telecommunication and home appliance industries (for gold-coated electrical connections)
- Satellite manufacturers (who use gold-plate shields and reflectors to protect equipment from solar radiation)
- The latest laser technology (used in medicine to perform eye operations and kill cancerous cells. The lasers use gold reflectors to concentrate light energy)
- Motor industry (for gold-coated contacts in sensors that activate air bags).

Many of these are "new technologies", at the cutting edge of industry. So without gold, the global economy and the lives of millions of people will be affected in some way.

I heard that 16 people were shot dead by the miners who wanted their land. These men know that it is illegal to enter the land of the Indians, but if there are no Indians ... what can you say?

I blame the garimpeiros. They cannot be controlled. At our mine, owned by a multi-national company, we obey government regulations. 96% of the mercury we use gets recycled. We try to contain our mercury waste and keep it out of the rivers.

Summary Questions

1 Make a list of the points for and against gold mining in the Amazon rainforest.

2 Summarise your own views on the issue of gold mining in the Amazon rainforest.

How Science Works

Smart electricity meters

The government would like to encourage people to use less electricity. One idea is to change everybody's electricity meters so that they are more aware of the energy that they use. If we knew how much it was costing us, we might think twice before switching on appliances that use a lot of energy.

How would these new electricity meters be different from the old ones?

- In most houses, the electricity meter is hidden away in a cupboard or under the stairs, or outside in a box where no-one ever looks.
- Some people have 'dual tariff' meters. These measure the electricity used at different times of the day. Electricity used at night is cheaper because there is less demand for it. People use cheaper, night-time electricity to run their washing machines and night storage heaters.
- The new 'smart' electricity meters would be in a prominent place in the house. They would show how much electricity was being used. They might also show how much it was costing. They might show when the tariff (price per unit) was more expensive so that consumers could avoid these times.

> **a** Why is electricity more expensive during the day?

- Do electricity costs vary?
- What is the impact on the environment of using electricity?
- What are the arguments for and against installing smart electricity meters?

We must get energy consumption down if we are to meet our targets for reducing carbon output. Once consumers can see how to manage their use of energy better, they will make great savings.

It will cost over £100 to install each new meter. Then people will buy less electricity from us. The government should pay for these new meters, not us.

We need to make much more use of renewables like wind power. Only then can we have an electricity supply which is sustainable into the future. And if we can reduce overall consumption, that would also be a great help.

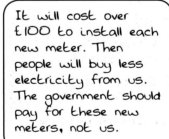

People should simply use less energy. They should switch appliances off unless they are absolutely essential. Encouraging people to use off-peak electricity may mean that they use more energy, not less.

I don't want the government or the electricity company putting some new meter into my house to tell me when I can and cannot switch the lights on.

We already have a 'smart meter' which tells me when it's an expensive time to use electricity. The little red light usually comes on during cold winter evenings. That warns me not to switch on the washing machine or the water heater because these things use a lot of power.

activity

Your task

Design a new-style electricity meter which will help consumers to be more aware of their electricity consumption.

- What will the meter look like and what will it show?
- Where will it be placed in the house?
- How will it help to save electricity?
- Once you have designed your new meter, you must design an advertising campaign to promote it.
- How will you convince people that the new meter will benefit them?

Summary Questions

1. Do you know anyone who uses 'Economy 7' or 'white meter' electricity? How does this work?

2. a) Which appliances use the most electricity?
   b) How much electricity do appliances use if they are left on stand-by?

3. a) Why do people use more electricity now than 20 years ago?
   b) Why are we encouraged to use less electricity?
   c) How could we have a sustainable electricity supply?

How Science Works

What career opportunities does science open up to me?

Careers and science

Using science as a large part of your job

People in a wide variety of jobs use science in some way or other. For some people science plays a major role in their workplace. They might have to:

- classify or identify things
- obtain or make things
- monitor and control changes.

These people will probably have qualifications in science. Many will think of themselves as 'scientists', although they might not wear white coats or work in a laboratory.

Look at the environmental scientist in the photo opposite. She is checking the quality of water in this river.

Not all scientists work in a lab

a Choose, from the three bullet points above, the statement that best describes what the environmental scientist in the photo is doing.

b Make a list of people who use science and/or scientific equipment as a large part of their job.

Using science as a small part of your job

There are many other people who use some science in their work but we don't think of them as scientists at all. For example, look at the pictures below:

c Name one other job, besides those shown above, that uses science, but not in a major way.

Interesting jobs

Choose one large company of your choice to investigate.

Try to find out:

- the types of scientific activity that are carried out
- the importance of the activity to society or the community
- the job titles and qualifications of the people who perform them
- the skills used by the people employed.

Summary Questions

1 a) Name one local, one national and one international company that use science.

  b) Find out where the organisations are located and why.

2 Make a list of skills that scientists need in addition to their qualifications.

3 Make a leaflet for a careers adviser showing the careers available in science and science-related areas.

Glossary

accelerate Speed up

accurate Describes data that is near to the true value

acid A chemical that can dissolve in water to make a solution with a pH of less than 7

acid rain Rain with a pH lower than that of natural rain water

activation energy The minimum energy needed for a chemical reaction to happen

addictive A substance which causes the body to have a physical craving

air resistance The force on an object, opposing its motion, as it travels through air

alcoholic A person who is addicted to alcohol

alkali A chemical that can dissolve in water to make a solution with a pH of more than 7

allele A version of a gene, e.g. blue eye, brown eye

alloy A solid mixture, made mainly of metals

analgesic A painkiller

anomalous A result that does not fit the pattern of the other results

anorexia nervosa An eating disorder where a person loses excessive weight through starvation

antibiotic A substance that damages pathogens without harming the patient

antibody A substance produced by white blood cells which damages pathogens in the body

antigen A substance that is part of a pathogen which triggers the white blood cells to make antibodies

antiseptic A substance that kills microbes on the skin and in wounds

area The number of square metres of a surface

arthritis A condition in which the joints become damaged and painful

atheroma A blockage on the walls of an artery

average speed The average distance travelled per second during a journey

bacterium A type of single-celled microbe

balanced Describes a lever when the turning effects in opposite directions cancel each other out

balanced forces Two or more forces whose effects cancel out

base A chemical which reacts with an acid to give a salt and water

binary fission The way cells reproduce by dividing in two

biofuel Fuel made from recently grown plants

branching diagram A type of key using a diagram with a series of options about the organism to be identified

bronchitis Infection of the bronchi in the lungs

cable A thick wire in which electric current flows to and from a device

carbon An element, which forms soot particles in cigarette smoke

carbon dioxide A gas that forms 0.04% of the air

carbon monoxide A toxic gas found in cigarette smoke

carbonate A metal compound that can react with an acid to form carbon dioxide, water and a salt

cardiovascular system The heart and blood vessels

catalyst A chemical that changes the rate of a chemical reaction, without being chemically changed itself at the end of the reaction

chemical potential energy The energy stored in a substance which is released in a chemical reaction

chromosome A structure found in a cell nucleus, made of DNA and comprising thousands of genes

cilia Small hair-like structures on the cells lining the lungs which remove mucus from the respiratory passages

cirrhosis Disease of the liver, often caused by alcoholism

clinical trial A way of testing drugs by comparing their effects with a placebo, a tablet containing no active ingredients

clone Organisms with identical genes

closed system A reaction where no extra reactants can get in, and no products can get out

combustion A chemical reaction that is also known as burning

continous variation A feature, such as height and weight, where individuals can be anywhere within a range

coronary thrombosis A blockage of an artery in the heart caused by a blood clot

corrosion A chemical change between oxygen and metal. Rust is an example of the result of corrosion

deficiency disease A disease caused by not having enough of a particular nutrient in the diet

depressant A drug which slows the body down

dicotyledon A broad-leafed plant

discontinuous variation A feature, such as sex, where individuals fit into one group or another

disinfectant A chemical used outside the body that kills microbes

displacement A reaction in which a more reactive element will displace a less reactive metal from its compound

distance travelled The distance travelled between starting and stopping

distance–time graph A graph representing motion by plotting distance travelled against time

dominant The 'stronger' allele of a gene which is outwardly apparent in a heterozygous individual

drag The force on an object, opposing its motion, as it travels through a liquid or a gas

drug A chemical which affects the way the body works

efficient Describes a change where little energy is wasted

effort The force exerted on a lever to move it

elastic potential energy The energy stored by an object which has been stretched or squashed

electrical energy The energy carried by an electric current

electricity meter A device used to measure energy supplied using electricity

electrolysis Using electricity to extract reactive metals from their ore

electron Very, very tiny particle which carries electricity through metals

emphysema A lung disease in which the walls of the alveoli are damaged, reducing the amount of oxygen which can be absorbed

endothermic A change that takes in energy

energy A variable measured in joules (J). It cannot be created or destroyed, only changed from one form to another

environmental Characteristics caused by the effects of where or how an organism lives

enzyme A molecule made of protein which controls chemical reaction in living things

epidemiology The study of how diseases are spread

evolution The gradual change in organisms from generation to generation through natural selection

exothermic A change that gives out energy

extraction Removing useful chemicals from raw materials

factor Anything which may have an effect on the outcome of an event or experiment

fluid A liquid or gas; any substance that flows

force A push or pull when two objects interact

fossil fuel Fuel which formed from living material a long time ago

fuel A substance whose stored energy is released in a usable form when it burns

fungus A microbe from the group which includes yeast, mushrooms and moulds

gamete A sex cell such as sperm, egg, pollen or ovules

gene A section of DNA carrying the instructions for a feature

generator A device which produces electricity when it is forced to turn

global warming Rise in average world temperatures over the 20th and 21st century, due to human pollution

goblet cell A type of cell found in the lining of the lung which makes mucus

gravitational potential energy The energy stored by an object which has been lifted up

greenhouse effect The natural effect of the atmosphere trapping radiated heat from the Earth to increase average world temperatures

hallucinogen A type of drug which causes people to see things that are not really there

hazardous Describes something which is dangerous

heat energy Energy travelling from a hotter place to a colder place

heating effect A material gets hot when an electric current passes through it

heterozygous An organism with different alleles of a gene

homozygous An organism with the same pair of alleles of a gene

hormone A chemical made in a gland which is carried in the blood and affects the activity of many parts of the body

hybrid A cross between two different but closely related species

hydrocarbon A chemical that contains only hydrogen and carbon. Often used as fuels

immune system The cells that defend us against microbes

immunisation Giving someone a vaccine to protect them against a disease

infection A disease caused by a microbe

inherited Characteristics passed on from parents in their genes

invertebrate An organism without a backbone

joule (J) The unit of energy

kinetic energy The energy of a moving object

kingdom One of the five largest groups in the classification of living things

kwashiorkor A form of malnutrition caused by a lack of protein

lever A pivoted device in which an applied force produces another force on an object

light gate A device which sends an electrical signal when a light beam is broken

load The force on a lever which must be overcome to make it move

lung cancer A lung disease, often caused by the tar in cigarette smoke

lymphocyte A white blood cell which makes antibodies

malnutrition Not having the correct balance of nutrients to stay healthy

metal A chemical that is shiny, malleable and a conductor. They often have high melting and boiling points and are sonorous

metal hydroxide A chemical that has a pH greater than 7 and can neutralise acids

metal oxide A compound of a metal and oxygen which is basic, i.e. it will react with an acidic solution

metal salt A chemical made when the hydrogen in an acid is swapped for a metal

microbe A living thing that can only be seen with a microscope

micro-organisms Organisms including bacteria, fungi, viruses and protozoa

mine A series of tunnels used to extract natural resources from the Earth

mineral (biology) A compound of an element which is essential for animals and/or plants to grow

mineral (chemistry) Elements or compounds found in rocks

model A way of thinking about something by comparing it with something more familiar

moment The turning effect of a force

monocotyledon A plant with narrow leaves, such as grasses

mucus A sticky liquid produced by the goblet cells which traps dirt and microbes in the lungs

natural selection The process by which favourable characteristics are passed on and less favourable characteristics disappear

neutralisation A chemical reaction between a base (or alkali) and an acid. This makes a metal salt and water

nicotine The addictive chemical found in cigarette smoke

non-renewable A natural resource that will run out

obese Being unhealthily overweight

open system A reaction where extra reactants can get in, and products can get out

ore A mineral that contains enough metal to allow money to be made if the metal is extracted

overdose Taking a large amount of a drug which can cause serious harm

oxidation A chemical reaction where a substance gains oxygen

oxidising agent A chemical that contains a lot of oxygen that it can give up in a chemical reaction

panning A method for extracting small particles of eroded native metals from a stream or river

parallel circuit An electric circuit in which some of the components are connected side-by-side

particle model A model of matter pictured as being made up of moving particles

penicillin The first antibiotic to be discovered

phagocyte A white blood cell which engilfs and digests pathogens

pivot The point about which a lever turns

pollution Changes to an ecosystem caused by humans. This could include changes to light, heat, noise, chemicals etc.

potential energy The energy which an object has in a particular position

power supply A source of electricity, used in the laboratory

precision A measurement of 12.04 mm has been made with greater precision than one of 12 mm

pressure The force acting per unit area (per square metre)

principle of moments A rule used in calculations involving levers

protozoan A type of microbe such as amoeba

quarry A large open air excavation in the Earth's surface, where natural materials are dug out

rancid Describes the product formed in the oxidation of fat

rate The speed of a chemical reaction

reactivity A suggestion of how likely a chemical is to undergo a chemical change

reactivity series A list of elements from the most reactive to the least reactive

recessive The 'weaker' allele of a gene which is not outwardly apparent in a heterozygous individual

recreational drug A drug which people take for pleasure (but which might be harmful)

reduction A chemical reaction where a substance loses oxygen

reliable Every time the experiment is repeated, the results are almost the same

renewable A natural resource that will not run out

resistance Tells us how easy or difficult it is for an electric current to pass through something

responsible Avoiding possible harmful consequences

rusting The corrosion of iron by water and oxygen to form hydrated iron oxide (rust)

salt See metal salt

seed An embryonic form of a plant, which contains a supply of food

selective breeding Choosing individuals with desirable characteristics to be parents of the next generation

series circuit An electric circuit in which all the components are connected end-to-end

slope of the graph How steep the line on a graph is

smelting Using a carbon displacement reaction to extract a metal from its ore

solution A type of mixture

solution displacement A more reactive metal will displace a less reactive metal from its compound that has been dissolved in water

species A group of organisms capable of interbreeding and producing fertile offspring

speed–time graph A graph representing motion by plotting speed against time

spontaneous A chemical reaction that happens without any extra energy being added

spore Similar to a seed, but without a store of food

stimulant A drug which speeds up the way the body works

streamlined An object shaped to reduce drag

stroke Damage caused by a blockage in an artery in the brain

systematic Describes when things are tried out in a planned and orderly way

tar A thick substance which causes cancer and which is present in cigarette smoke

taxonomic classification Sorting animals and plants into groups

terminal The point at which electrical connections are made

Theory of Conservation of Mass This states that the mass of reactants equals the mass of the products

therapeutic drug A drug which is used to treat patients

thermite A mixture of chemicals for a solid displacement reaction

time taken The amount of time between something starting and stopping

transition metal An element found in the middle block of the Periodic Table

transmitted When a disease is passed from one person to another

turbine A blade which is forced to turn by moving air, steam or water

turning effect The effect of a force on a lever; a bigger force further from the pivot has a greater turning effect

unbalanced forces Two or more forces whose effects do not cancel out

unethical Against moral ideas about what is right and wrong

unit of alcohol A measure of the amount of alcohol in drinks

unsustainable Describes something we do which uses up a natural resource

upthrust The upward force on an object in a liquid or gas

vaccination Giving someone a vaccine to protect them against a disease

vaccine Material from a pathogen which is given to people to make them produce antibodies

variation Differences between members of the same species

varieties A type of animal, or especially plant, which differs from others of the same species

Venn diagram A diagram that sorts items into groups, sub-groups and overlapping groups

vertebrate An animal with a backbone

virus The smallest type of microbe

vitamin A type of nutrient which is required in small amounts

weight The downward force on an object caused by gravity

white blood cell Type of blood cell, including lymphocytes and phagocytes

xylem A type of cell forming tubes, which carry water and minerals from the soil to the leaves of a plant

Index

Acknowledgements

Alamy 6.1, 6.3, 37.6, 45.6, 56.1, 56.2, 70.2, 71.5, 76.2, 80.4, 82.1, 116.2, 150.1; **Bruce Coleman** 75.4; **Charles Winters** 60.2; **Corbis** 15.3, 31.3, 45.5; **Fotolia** 3.2, 35.7, 37.3, 37.7, 38.2, 38.4, 41.5, 46.1, 46.4, 49.3, 68.1, 70.4, 74.2, 88.4, 91.3, 93.2, 98.1, 113.3, 120.4, 124.1, 131.3, 132.1; **Getty** 104.2, 133.5; **iStock** 3.3, 7.4, 12.1, 16.3, 16.5, 16.4, 16.2, 18.2, 18.3, 20.2, 21.3, 30.1, 33.9, 33.5, 33.3, 33.6, 37.1, 37.2, 37.5, 38.1, 38.3, 44.1, 44.2, 46.3, 78.2, 88.1, 90.1, 93.3, 98.2, 100.1, 100.2, 120.2, 120.3, 126.1, 128.1, 128.2, 128.3, 130.1, 131.4, 135.3, 136.1; **Martyn Chillmaid** 62.1, 62.2, 62.3, 86.1, 88.3; **NASA** 86.3; **Photolibrary** 7.5, 16.1, 33.2, 33.7, 33.8; **Geoff Covey** 33.4; **Science Photo Library** 6.2, 8.1, 8.2, 9.3, 9.4, 11.3, 11.4, 13.4, 13.5, 18.4, 18.5, 19.7, 19.8, 20.1, 21.5, 21.4, 24.1, 25.2, 28.1, 21.5, 21.4, 24.1, 25.2, 28.1, 30.2, 34.2, 35.6, 37.4, 37.8, 40.1, 46.2, 47.6, 49.5, 51.3, 55.3, 56.3, 66.2, 68.2, 68.4, 68.5, 70.1, 70.3, 72.1, 76.1, 78.1, 80.1, 82.2, 88.5, 96.1, 101.4, 102.1, 104.1, 106.1, 109.3, 111.4, 112.2, 114.3, 116.1, 121.5, 121.6, 129.5; **Science Enhancement Programme** 104.4, 104.5, 109.5, 110.3.

Picture research by GreenGate Publishing

Every effort has been made to trace all the copyright holders, but if any have been overlooked the publisher will be pleased to make the necessary arrangements at the first opportunity.